T0288948

AFTER THE WAR

NATION-BUILDING FROM
FDR TO GEORGE W. BUSH

JAMES DOBBINS, MICHELE A. POOLE,
AUSTIN LONG, BENJAMIN RUNKLE

Prepared for the Carnegie Corporation of New York

NATIONAL SECURITY
RESEARCH DIVISION

... published by ...

... the RAND Corporation ...
... objective analysis and effective solutions ...
... the public and private sectors around the world. RAND's ...
... publications do not necessarily reflect the opinions of its research ...
RAND® is a registered trademark.

To order RAND documents or to obtain additional information, contact
Distribution Services: Telephone: (310) 451-7002;
Fax: (310) 451-6915; Email: order@rand.org

Preface

Beginning with the post–World War II occupations of Germany and Japan, the United States has undertaken eight significant nation-building operations over the past 60 years. The planning for postwar nation-building in Germany and Japan began under President Franklin D. Roosevelt and was carried out under President Harry S. Truman. Subsequent operations during the post–Cold War era were initiated and conducted by President George H. W. Bush and President William J. Clinton, respectively. The United States has subsequently taken the lead in post–September 11, 2001, nation-building under President George W. Bush in Afghanistan and Iraq. In each of the eight cases presented here, presidential decisionmaking and administrative structure have, at times, worked in favor of the nation-building goals of the U.S. government and military and those of its coalition partners and allies. In other cases, these elements have hindered the achievement of these goals or have had negative effects on nation-building outcomes.

This monograph assesses the ways in which the management styles and structures of the administrations in power prior to and during nation-building operations affect the goals and outcomes of such operations. It also evaluates the nature of the society being reformed and of the conflict being terminated. The findings presented here should be of interest to policymakers and others interested in the history of U.S. nation-building, lessons learned from these operations, and the outcomes of U.S. involvement in rebuilding various types of societies.

This research was conducted within the International Security and Defense Policy Center of the RAND National Security Research Division (NSRD). NSRD conducts research and analysis for the Office of the Secretary of Defense, the Joint Staff, the Unified Combatant Commands, the defense agencies, the Department of the Navy, the Marine Corps, the U.S. Coast Guard, the U.S. Intelligence Community, allied foreign governments, and foundations. Support for this study was provided by the Carnegie Corporation of New York.

For more information on RAND's International Security and Defense Policy Center, contact the Director, James Dobbins. He can be reached by email at James_Dobbins@rand.org; by phone at 703-413-1100, extension 5134; or by mail at the RAND Corporation, 1200 S. Hayes Street, Arlington, VA 22202. More information about RAND is available at www.rand.org.

Contents

Figure

Summary

Winning wars and securing the peace are preeminent responsibilities of the U.S. defense and foreign-policy apparatus. In recent decades, the United States' overwhelming military superiority has allowed it to "overawe" or overrun adversaries with comparative ease. Consolidating victory and preventing a renewal of conflict has, by contrast, usually taken more time, energy, and resources than originally foreseen. Few recent efforts of this sort can be regarded as unqualified successes, and one or two must be considered clear failures.

In previous RAND research, we have explored the various factors that contribute to the success or failure of such missions. First among these is the nature of the society being reformed and of the conflict being terminated. Also important are the quality and quantity of the military and civil assets being brought to bear by external actors. And finally, there is the wisdom and skill with which these resources are applied.

This volume looks at the last of these influences. It examines, in particular, the manner in which U.S. policy toward postconflict reconstruction has been created and implemented and the effect that these processes have had on mission outcomes. We start with a review of the post–World War II occupations of Germany and Japan. The end of the Cold War brought a second spate of such missions—in Somalia, Haiti, Bosnia, and Kosovo. In the current decade, the terrorist attacks of September 11, 2001, have given rise to ongoing operations in Afghanistan and Iraq.

Presidential personality obviously influences the U.S. government's decisionmaking process in terms of approaches to and the conduct of reconstruction efforts: Each president will have specific preferences for oral or written interactions, different appetites for detail, and varying tolerance for conflict among and with subordinates. In examining the eight cases addressed here, which cover three historical periods, we consider the personal styles of five U.S. presidents, the processes by which they made decisions, and the structures through which these were given effect. The resultant approaches to decisionmaking are categorized by reference to certain archetypal modes, including the formalistic, the competitive, and the collegial. The first approach, often associated with Dwight D. Eisenhower, emphasizes order and hierarchy. The second, epitomized by Franklin Delano Roosevelt, seeks wisdom through the clash of ideas among competing subordinates. The third, identified with George H. W. Bush, encourages greater cooperation among presidential advisers. As these examples suggest, all three models can yield excellent results. They can also, as will become evident, produce quite unsatisfactory outcomes. This monograph examines successful and unsuccessful approaches to decisionmaking in the field of nation-building, with a view to identifying those combinations of style, process, and structure that seem to have worked best.

Post–World War II Nation-Building

The occupations of Germany and Japan were planned under Franklin D. Roosevelt and executed under Harry Truman. It is difficult to imagine two more different personalities: the first a worldly aristocrat, debonair, secretive, and informal, and the second a Midwestern machine politician prepared to delegate but ready to take responsibility. Roosevelt was the last U.S. president to function without a formal structure for the conduct of national security policy. Truman introduced the system under which the U.S. government operates today.

Despite these differences, there was a great deal of continuity between the two administrations. Truman kept many of Roosevelt's cabinet and subcabinet officials. He was also able to draw on a number of highly talented military and former military leaders who had matured in command of the United States' immense war effort, such as Douglas

MacArthur, Dwight D. Eisenhower, and George Marshall. Truman also inherited and worked within the intellectual framework set by his predecessor, putting his own stamp on U.S. policy only gradually, over time. Roosevelt integrated military and diplomatic considerations in his mind in a more informal manner. Truman established formal structures to bring together the military and civil aspects of his administration. Both listened to conflicting advice and tried to ensure that all relevant actors were heard from before making significant decisions.

The German and Japanese occupations remain the gold standard for postwar reconstruction. No subsequent nation-building effort has achieved comparable success. There are a number of reasons for this. Both Germany and Japan were highly homogeneous societies (in the German case, as a result of Nazi genocide and the enormous population transfers that occurred at the close of World War II). Both were industrialized economies. Both had been devastatingly defeated, and both had surrendered unconditionally. Few of these conditions were replicated in future cases.

The scale of U.S. power was also greater in 1945 than at any time before or since. At war's end, 1.7 million U.S. soldiers were garrisoned in the American sector of Germany, in which there were only 17 million Germans—a ratio of one foreign soldier to every 10 inhabitants. At that point, the United States was producing and consuming half the entire world's annual product. It was also the world's only nuclear power, having just dropped two such weapons on Japanese cities.

If the German and Japanese occupations were alike in outcome, they were very different in execution. In Japan, the strategy was one of co-option, with nearly all elements of the Japanese government retained and reformed from within. In Germany, the approach was exactly the opposite. Every national institution was abolished and rebuilt anew several years later. The former approach proved simpler and faster; the latter was ultimately more thorough.

In both cases, U.S. occupation policy was extensively planned and skillfully executed. Roosevelt had been reluctant to make decisions about postwar policy as long as the fighting continued, but extensive, if not fully coordinated, preparations had nevertheless been made with the involvement of the U.S. Department of State (DOS) and the

U.S. Department of the Treasury, as well as the military services. With 9 million troops under arms and a defense budget approaching 40 percent of gross domestic product, the United States also had a very capable instrument with which to carry out its intentions. Those intentions changed substantially in response to a changing international climate as the occupations continued. Nevertheless, the original plans and their implementing structures proved flexible enough to accommodate these changes successfully, and the new system established by Truman for the integration of the civil and military aspects of national security policy provided necessary guidance.

Roosevelt had been president for nearly 10 years when the war began and the nation's responsibilities vastly expanded. His approach to administration relied on a combination of intuition and experience, allowing him to govern effectively through a very informal, conflictual, and personalized approach. In contrast, the Truman administration took a more structured approach. Accordingly, Truman created the system embodied in the National Security Act of 1947 that remains in effect today.[1]

Post–Cold War Nation-Building

Throughout the Cold War, most U.S. military interventions involved either "hot" wars, such as those in Korea and Vietnam, or relatively brief incursions, such as those in the Dominican Republic, Lebanon, Grenada, and Panama. Many international disputes were left unresolved, lest their resolution upset the East-West balance. Berlin, Germany, Europe, Cyprus, Palestine, Korea, and China all remained divided, and either U.S. or United Nations (UN) forces policed and maintained those divisions. The goal of such interventions was not nation-building but the policing of cease-fires and the suppression of renewed conflict.

With the end of the Cold War, it became possible to secure broad international support for and participation in efforts to end festering conflicts and impose enduring peace. Nation-building, after a 40-year

---

[1]   See Public Law 80-235, National Security Act of 1947, July 26, 1947.

hiatus, came back into vogue. The UN embarked on a number of such missions in the 1990s, and the United States led four. The first began under George H. W. Bush; the next three were conducted under the William Jefferson Clinton administration.

The elder Bush and Clinton were also a study in contrasts. Bush had a slightly stiff patrician style and a seemingly unbeatable resume, having served in Congress, as head of the Central Intelligence Agency (CIA), as ambassador to China, and as Ronald Reagan's vice president. His decisionmaking style was formal, collegial, and methodical. Clinton was an outgoing populist with no federal and scant international experience. He initially favored a highly unstructured and informal style of decisionmaking but adopted an increasingly staff-driven approach after early embarrassing setbacks revealed the inadequacies of his initial approach to governance.

Unlike Truman, Clinton did not profit from his predecessor's accumulated expertise. Coming as he did from a different party, one that had been out of executive office for 12 years, Clinton filled his staff and his cabinet with new faces, few of them with substantial executive-branch experience.

The elder Bush had proved himself a master statesman in dealing with the twilight of a world familiar to him, the Cold War era. He and his team proved less adept at dealing with the challenges of the new world order, or disorder, that replaced the old. Under Bush's leadership, the United States helped reunify Germany, liberate Eastern Europe, and deal with the disintegration of the Soviet Union. It also stood aside as Yugoslavia descended into civil war. Responding to mounting famine in Somali, Bush mounted a humanitarian rescue mission there that, while successful in its own terms, contained none of the elements that might have helped secure an enduring peace.

Clinton's initial inclination was to act as his own chief of staff, both dipping into the details and exploring broad lines of policy, satisfying his wide-ranging curiosity and exercising his formidable ability to establish personal contacts. These energies were initially focused on domestic policy, with the status of homosexuals in the military being his first, poorly chosen foray into national security policy. The U.S. military effort in Somalia remained on autopilot, steered by junior officials while their superiors oriented themselves to new jobs and an unfamiliar international environment.

Under Bush, the United States had sent a relatively large and capable force to Somalia to execute a very limited mission: protecting the delivery of food and medicine to a starving population. Under Clinton, the United States reduced that military presence from 20,000 to 2,000 soldiers and gave this residual force the mission of supporting a UN-led program of grassroots democratization that was bound to antagonize Somali warlords. This mismatch of soaring objectives and plummeting capabilities caught up to the ill-fated mission in a firefight in downtown Mogadishu, memorialized in the book and movie *Blackhawk Down*. Shortly thereafter, Clinton announced that he would withdraw all U.S. forces within six months. A year later, the rest of the UN troops left as well, having achieved nothing of lasting value.

This and other early missteps led Clinton to replace both his chief of staff and his secretary of defense. The rest of his national security team became much more cautious and methodical in planning subsequent military expeditions, recognizing that they could lose their jobs and their reputations through inattention or ill-considered action. Clinton himself never gave up his fascination with the details of policy nor his penchant for personal engagement, but he did rely much more heavily on White House staff to run a disciplined interagency process, conduct methodical planning, and generate carefully considered options for his review.

As a result, the design and execution of nation-building missions improved. The Haiti intervention in 1994 was entirely successful within the limited parameters that had been set for it—restore a freely elected president to office, oversee elections to choose his successor, and then leave. Unfortunately, this was too narrow a mission with too limited a time span to repair a society as profoundly broken as Haiti's. The United States achieved all its stated objectives, left after two years, and had to intervene again a decade later.

In 1995, after sending U.S. forces into Bosnia, Clinton again pledged an early departure, but by 1996, he had learned enough to renege on the promise. This intervention was the result of a long and painful process of transatlantic and East-West consultations, the very nature of which compelled a considerable degree of planning and fore-thought. Although the resultant stabilization strategy had to be mod-ified over subsequent years, this lengthy process of gestation helped ensure that those responsible for executing the mission had the per-sonnel, money, and broad international backing necessary to do so successfully.

Kosovo was the last and best prepared of the Clinton interven-tions. The air war lasted longer than intended but achieved its objec-tives without a single allied casualty. Serb forces abandoned Kosovo, and North Atlantic Treaty Organization (NATO) troops came in behind them. Security was quickly established, and the UN set up a provisional administration. Within a few weeks, nearly all of the more than 1 million Muslim refugees and displaced persons returned to their homes, and a much smaller number of ethnic Serbs departed.

Clinton's improving performance in the field of nation-building had much to do with the increasingly methodical process by which these missions were planned. Clinton himself retained ultimate author-ity and never gave the final go-ahead until convinced that no option short of the dispatch of U.S. troops would suffice. This uncertainty over the President's ultimate willingness to launch an operation was a source of considerable frustration to those urging military action. The effect, however, was to allow for an extended debate between the advo-cates of such action, usually in DOS, and opponents, usually in the U.S. Department of Defense (DoD), regarding the wisdom and shape of these operations. As a result, every downside to intervention that its opponents could conceive was considered, every alternative they could offer was explored, and every assumption they questioned was sub-jected to examination.

Clinton was also successful in leveraging relatively modest U.S. troop and financial commitments to secure much larger international engagements. The United States provided less than a quarter of NATO forces in Bosnia and less than a sixth of those in Kosovo. Its finan-cial contribution to the two operations was commensurately low. No one doubted that these were U.S.-led interventions—ones that would not have taken place absent Washington's leadership—but they were also heavily multinational in character, with NATO, the UN, the

Organization for Security and Co-Operation in Europe (OSCE), the World Bank, and other international organizations playing major roles. The result was enhanced legitimacy and lowered cost, achieved at the expense of some sharing of authority and responsibility.

Neither of the Balkan interventions brought about transformations of the sort made in post–World War II Germany and Japan. Christians and Muslims, Serbs and Croats remained mutually suspicious. Politics continued to be organized along ethnic lines. But politics, not armed conflict, became the field in which competition for wealth and power was played out, and this pacification was, fundamentally, what the interventions had sought to achieve. Bosnia and Kosovo are not yet self-sustained polities, but U.S. troops are entirely out of the former, and only a few hundred remain in the latter, and both societies are headed toward eventual membership in the European Union

Clinton's opponents in Congress spent much of the 1990s criticizing both the conduct and the fact of his nation-building activity. Some of this criticism was ill informed—that these deployments were harming readiness, enlistment, and retention, for instance—but the overall effect was not entirely unconstructive. Faced with a skeptical Congress, the administration needed to constantly demonstrate that its efforts were enhancing security and promoting political and economic reform in these societies. Such claims were critically scrutinized and sometimes shown to be exaggerated. Thus, the administration was kept constantly on its toes.

A more pernicious effect of this criticism was to discourage efforts to institutionalize the conduct of such missions. Many in the U.S. defense establishment saw nation-building as a diversion from what they believed to be their real purpose, which was to fight and win conventional wars, a view that was reinforced by their congressional overseers. Accordingly, there was little effort to develop a coherent doctrine for the conduct of such operations or to build a cadre of experts who would be available from one mission to the next. DOS also tended to treat each successive mission as an exceptional, not-to-be-repeated demand on its resources. Only the White House restructured itself to take on these new tasks, and these changes proved transient. A directorate was created within the National Security Council to handle the

planning and coordination of what were called, somewhat euphemis-
tically, *complex contingency operations*, *nation-building* having become
a term of opprobrium. In 1997, Clinton issued Presidential Decision
Directive (PDD) 56, which established an interagency structure and
mandated a set of procedures for the future planning and conduct of
such operations.[2]

Post-9/11 Nation-Building

George W. Bush retained Clinton's interagency machinery largely
intact, though, naturally, he replaced most of the senior players. He
entirely dismantled the prior administration's nation-building component, however. A directive that would have replaced and, indeed,
extended and improved on PDD 56 was drafted by the new National
Security Council staff but quashed by the Pentagon. The failure of
Condoleezza Rice, the new National Security Advisor, to persist in getting the directive issued may have reflected an expectation that no new
nation-building would be initiated on her watch, given the negative
attitude that she and Bush had expressed toward such activity during
the recent presidential campaign.

This attitude changed as a result of the September 11, 2001,
attacks on New York and Washington, but it did so only slowly. If
the Bush administration was to reconstruct, first, Afghanistan and,
then, Iraq, it would do so with an eagerness to distinguish its conduct from that of the preceding administration. Whereas, following
the debacle of Somalia and the disappointing results in Haiti, Clinton
had abandoned quick exit strategies, embraced the Powell doctrine of
overwhelming force, sought the broadest possible multilateral participation, and accepted the need for long-term commitment to societies
it was trying to reform and rebuild, George W. Bush remained wary
of long-term entanglements, emphasized economy of force, was skeptical of multilateral institutions, and envisaged an initially quite limited
role for the United States in rebuilding and reforming the countries it
occupied.

---

[2] See Presidential Decision Directive 56, Managing Complex Contingency Operations,
May 1997.

Secretary of Defense Donald Rumsfeld was most explicit in explaining this new approach. In speeches and newspaper articles, he argued that, by flooding Bosnia and Kosovo with troops and money, the United States and its allies had turned both societies into permanent wards of the international community. By limiting U.S. engagement in Afghanistan and Iraq, in terms of military personnel, economic assistance, and duration, the Bush administration intended to ensure that those two counties achieved self-sufficiency much more quickly.

In Afghanistan, this low-profile, small-footprint philosophy was applied with considerable rigor, making this mission the least resourced U.S.-led nation-building operations in modern history. On a per capita basis, Bosnia, for instance, had received 50 times more international military personnel and 16 times more economic assistance than did Afghanistan over the first couple of years of reconstruction. In Afghanistan, the administration refused to use U.S. troops for peacekeeping and opposed the deployment of international forces outside the capital for the same purpose. Security was to remain a responsibility of the Afghans, despite the fact that the country had neither army nor police forces. Not surprisingly, Afghanistan became more—not less—dependent on external assistance as the years went by.

Nation-building in Iraq was more heavily resourced than in Afghanistan, but, otherwise, the break with past practice was even more radical. Only weeks before the invasion, President Bush transferred responsibility for overseeing all the nonmilitary aspects of the occupation from DOS to DoD. For the first time in more than 50 years, there would be no U.S. diplomatic mission working alongside U.S. forces in a postconflict environment. Rejecting the division of labor developed in Korea, Vietnam, the Dominican Republic, Lebanon, Grenada, Panama, Somalia, Haiti, Bosnia, Kosovo, and Afghanistan, the administration chose to revert to an organizational model similar to that last employed in Germany and Japan 50 years earlier. DoD, not DOS, would oversee both democratization and economic development, including agricultural reform, the resumption of oil exports, the creation of a new currency, the setting of tariffs, the creation of a free media, the promotion of civil society, the establishment of political parties, the drafting of a constitution, and the organization of elections—all activities with which DoD had little modern experience.

The reasons for this decision seemed persuasive at the time: Bush had become frustrated with the slow pace of reconstruction in Afghanistan, a failure that he attributed to poor interagency coordination rather than to a paucity of resources. There was also a sense that civil-military wrangling had interfered with implementation of the Dayton accord in Bosnia in the mid-1990s. Perhaps also sensing that DOS had reservations about the wisdom of invading Iraq, Bush decided to put all aspects of the operation under DoD, thereby ensuring unity of command and unreserved commitment to the mission. However, DoD proved poorly equipped to assume the new responsibilities thrust upon it. The Coalition Provisional Authority (CPA), established under DoD auspices to govern Iraq, was never close to fully staffed, and most of those working in it remained for only a few months. Many of CPA administrator Paul Bremer's most senior advisers came from other agencies, but there were never enough, and the expertise below this level dropped sharply. What institutional memory the U.S. government retained in the field of nation-building thus remained largely untapped. The result was a long series of unforeseen challenges and hastily improvised responses.

Most of the early decisions that shaped the Afghanistan and Iraq operations were eventually reversed, but only after the operations conclusively failed to achieve their objectives. Beginning in late 2003, personnel and financial commitments to Afghanistan were doubled and redoubled, then redoubled again, only to barely keep pace with the mounting threat of a resurgent Taliban. In Iraq, civil tasks were returned to DOS, and a diplomatic mission was opened in 2004. Civilian staffing remained a problem, but never to the extent that had plagued the CPA. Troop levels were raised, more sophisticated counterinsurgency tactics were introduced, and a dialogue was initiated with neighboring governments, including Iran. By the end of 2007, the security situation had begun to improve, though the possibility of an even wider civil war loomed, with both Sunni and Shia better organized and more heavily armed than they had been a year earlier.

In the immediate aftermath of 9/11, the Bush administration's decisionmaking processes worked well. Indeed, despite the necessary lack of any forward planning, the Afghan campaign of 2001 provided a textbook illustration of the successful integration of force and diplomacy in terms of national power and international legitimacy. Every U.S. government agency involved worked toward a common goal with minimal friction. The CIA ran paramilitary operations, DoD ran the military, and DOS oversaw the diplomacy. Each deferred to the others in their spheres of competence. The CIA put together an overall strategy for the war and guided the application of U.S. military power in support of local anti-Taliban insurgents. That agency also put U.S. diplomats in contact with key Afghan actors. The devastating effect of U.S. air power gave decisive weight to U.S. diplomacy. Nearly universal international support gave that diplomacy added influence. As a result, operating from a standing start, the United States was able to both displace the Taliban and replace it with a representative, moderate, domestically popular, and internationally recognized regime within a matter of weeks.

The absence of an existing structure or agreed-upon doctrine for the conduct of postconflict reconstruction was not immediately felt. There was not time for elaborate planning, and the administration had, in any case, no intention of engaging in large-scale nation-building. Once it found itself embroiled in such an enterprise, however, its lack of plans and the absence of any consensus on how to proceed became more debilitating. Each agency blamed the other for the lack of progress, with DOS arguing that there could be no development without security, DoD making the opposite case, and the President becoming increasingly frustrated. One response might have been for him to empower the White House staff to play a more forceful role in setting and ensuring the implementation of reconstruction policy. Instead, with war in Iraq looming, he turned over responsibility for coordinating the interagency effort to DoD.

In doing so, he effectively took himself and his staff out of the loop. Policies were set and direction given by the Secretary of Defense and his staff or at the initiative of the CPA administrator in Iraq. For half a year, there was no structured debate among cabinet-level officers on Iraq policy, nor were contentious issues put to the President for resolution. Indeed, for the first few months, reports from Iraq were not even shared with other agencies or the White House. Decisions that would to fundamentally shape the occupation, including the disbandment of the army, the exclusion tens of thousands of former regime officials from office, and the timetable for elections were made and announced without formal interagency review. It was not until late 2003 that the White House staff resumed its role of running the interagency process, overseeing presidential decisionmaking, and coordinating the relevant agencies to ensure their implementation.

Presidential style had much do with the resultant process. George W. Bush practiced a top-down, inspirational mode of leadership that did not invite dissent or welcome extensive debate. He preferred to maximize control, minimize leaks, and maintain message discipline at the expense of the sort of give and take among his chief advisers that might have yielded more informed choices and better considered decisions. The result was unprecedented public support for the initial military campaigns in both Afghanistan and Iraq but poor planning and inept implementation of the postconflict strategy. Blame for these lapses has sometimes been attributed to Condoleezza Rice, the President's young, and, in comparison with her Cabinet-level colleagues, less experienced, National Security Advisor. It seems likely, however, that President Bush received the interagency process that he wanted. His failure, for instance, to solicit the views of the Secretary of Defense, the Secretary of State, or the Director of the CIA before deciding to invade Iraq was almost certainly a calculated choice on his part, not an oversight on the part of his staff, as was the decision to transfer to the Secretary of Defense the responsibility for integrating other agency efforts and views during the occupation of Iraq. Both choices would seem to reflect a low tolerance for discord among subordinates and a limited appetite for mastering the level of detail that would have allowed him to effectively adjudicate disputes among them.

In early 2007, President Bush acted contrary to the initial recommendations of many of his senior civilian and military advisers to significantly increase U.S. troop strength in Iraq. In this instance, Bush does seem to have consulted widely within and outside the National Security Council, giving all major stakeholders an opportunity to express their views. Whether this more comprehensive and methodical process of consultation was the result of experience or simply the product of his weakened political position is unclear. In any case, the decision to surge troop levels in Iraq, in conjunction with other factors, did result in a significant reduction of violence there. This experience suggests that, while a president need not adhere to advisers' recommendations, the result of seeking such advice may be better decisions and a more wholehearted implementation.

Conclusions

Successful nation-building requires unity of effort across multiple agencies and, often, multiple governments. Decisionmaking structures thus need to provide for a combination of common effort and unified direction. The entire national security establishment needs to be engaged. This is not a responsibility that presidents can afford to delegate, nor is it one that any single department of government can handle. Indeed, the requirement to include not just other agencies but also other governments and international organizations in modern nation-building enterprises makes any replication of the post–World War II viceroy model epitomized by Douglas MacArthur in Japan highly unrealistic.

Washington's decisionmaking structures need to reflect an appropriate balance between a well-structured, deliberative process and the varying styles of an individual president. The Clinton-era PDD 56 provides one possible template. However much it was followed during that administration, the process as outlined therein at least gave guidance to what "right" decisionmaking would look like, creating expectations of orderly debate and thorough planning that were largely met as long as it remained in force.

The key element of any decisionmaking process is structured debate within one or more senior interagency groups that include all relevant agencies. This will mean, at a minimum, the involvement of DoD and DOS, along with the CIA (in an advisory rather than policy-making capacity, though the line between the two is seldom distinct). These groups provide a forum for the airing of divergent views and should be tasked with creating a range of options and likely scenarios. Members should be allowed significant latitude to disagree in this initial period. In effect, this is an attempt to institutionalize the "collegial" model of decisionmaking.

Of particular importance is this model's emphasis on lateral communication. Unfortunately, this can depend heavily on the personalities involved. Parochial tendencies often limit willingness and ability to communicate. Steps to establish a certain level of interagency comfort could facilitate such communication. One possible way to foster this comfort would be to require cross- or interagency tours for those seeking senior positions within civilian agencies, much as the military services require a joint assignment for promotion.

Once the president chooses or endorses a particular option, a fully integrated political-military plan should be generated. This is tricky, because the same type of interagency group that was given free range to debate and dissent must now be tasked with drafting and executing a single plan that may be an alternative to which some were strenuously opposed in the initial phase of decisionmaking. Regardless, it is important that all relevant players be included in implementation planning and execution.

Civil-military integration means having civilian agencies give advice on war plans and having the military comment on diplomacy. This will undoubtedly be painful; the military doubtless does not want to hear the U.S. Agency for International Development's (USAID's) view on target selection any more than USAID wants to hear the military's view on the utility of public-works projects in combat zones. However, advice does not equal final authority; serious disputes will have to be aired and resolved by senior leaders, including the president, if necessary. It is better that such disputes be ironed out before nation-building begins rather than in its midst.

While integrated political-military planning is important, so is establishing a clear and enduring division of labor for various aspects of nation-building. It is a bureaucratic truism that "when all are responsible for an issue, none takes responsibility." In other words, a lack of clear responsibility is a recipe for buck-passing and indecision.

For the past 15 years, critical functions, such as overseeing military and police training, providing humanitarian and reconstruction aid, and promoting democratic development have been repeat-

xxvi   After the War: Nation-Building from FDR to George W. Bush

edly transferred from DOS to DoD and back again. This has left each agency uncertain of its long-term responsibilities and, consequently, disinclined to invest in improving its performance.

The United States thus needs to decide whether nation-building is going to be an enduring part of its repertoire. If so, it will need to rebalance the political and the military elements of national power. For example, the Army and the Marine Corps are projected to add about 90,000 troops to their end strength over the next several years. Despite recent and projected future expansion, the total number of personnel in civilian agencies associated with nation-building, including USAID, the CIA, and DOS, is dwarfed by this number. Budgets are similarly weighted toward the military. Absent some effort to redress this imbalance and to create an operational civilian cadre for nation-building, the implementation of U.S. policy in this field is likely to remain stunted no matter how good the quality of its decisionmaking.

If DOS and USAID are to receive more funding and personnel to perform these functions, those personnel will need to be available when required. It is not realistic to think that domestic civil servants can be sent involuntarily into a war zone. U.S. Foreign Service personnel, however, are already subject, in theory at least, to worldwide availability. This practice of directed assignments has largely lapsed since thousands of DOS and USAID officers were sent to Vietnam. It will have to be revitalized if these agencies are to secure and retain the higher funding and personnel levels that their nation-building responsibilities require

Setbacks in Iraq and a sense that U.S. leadership is faltering worldwide have led some to argue that the entire interagency structure first given form in 1947 is outdated. The world, it is argued, is a far more complex place today, and the U.S. government is much larger. In fact, however, the world is not more chaotic today than it was in 1947, and the federal government is not all that much larger. One has only to recall the incredible turbulence that affected the international system in the decade after World War II, with the fall of the Iron Curtain, the "loss" of China, and the disintegration of the British and French colonial empires, to put today's challenges into perspective. It is true that information moves much more quickly today, and the federal government has many more civilian employees and fewer military personnel than it did 60 years ago. Neither of these factors necessarily makes policy harder to formulate and execute.

In fact, the current system for integrating defense and foreign policy has actually functioned quite well for most of the past 60 years. It helped win the Cold War, unite Europe, cope with the collapse of the Soviet Union, deal with the early challenges of the post–Cold War era, and respond to the attacks of 9/11. A system that was working adequately only six years ago is probably not irretrievably broken today. As this study illustrates, many of what are now considered flawed decisions of the past several years were made not because the interagency system was defective but, rather, because it was circumvented or neglected.

That said, there are improvements that would strengthen the capacity of the current system to deal successfully with the intense interagency and international integration required for successful nation-building. Legislation to establish an enduring division of labor among DOS, DoD, USAID, and other agencies engaged in these missions would promote the development of a more professional approach to nation-building, as would a provision to require a tour of service in a national security agency other than one's own for entry into the senior executive staff and foreign service. Legislation to set aside a certain proportion of subcabinet and White House staff positions for career officers would also help sustain the learning curve from one administration to the next.

Whatever approach to decisionmaking presidents may adopt— formal, competitive, collegial, or some combination thereof—it is important that they foster debate among their principal advisers and value disciplined dissent as an essential aid to wise decisionmaking. It is equally important that presidents and their principal advisers have access to professional, experienced staff. Once decisions are made, these need to be implemented, to the extent possible, through established structures, employing tried methodologies and respecting existing lines of authority. Most bureaucratic innovation comes at significant cost in terms of immediately degraded performance, whatever its long-term effect. Institutional improvisation may be necessary to cope with new challenges. Nation-building, however, is a familiar and repetitive requirement—one that requires greater consistency of method and transmission of expertise from one administration to the next than the system has so far achieved.

It should come as no surprise that administrations get better at policy formulation and execution as they progress. Neither can it come as a shock that much of this acquired experience is not passed from one administration to the next, particularly when the successor is drawn from the opposing party. Nevertheless, the degree to which the U.S. government has experienced a regression of competence in the field of nation-building from one administration the next should be a source of real concern. Obstacles to the transmission of expertise thus need to be identified and, where possible, leveled.

Two modern administrations are often held up as exemplars of orderly process and sound policy under exceptionally challenging circumstances. Harry Truman set U.S. strategy for the conduct of the Cold War, and George H. W. Bush brought it to a successful conclusion. Both had been vice president and had considerable experience in Washington. Both succeeded presidents of their own party. Truman took office at the opening of the Cold War, in the 13th year of a Democratic administration, and he retained, in one capacity or another, many members of his predecessor's national security team. Bush succeeded Reagan, also a Republican. Neither Truman nor Bush had campaigned against his predecessor's record, and neither administration felt obligated to do things differently simply to disassociate itself from what had come before. The quality of both presidencies profited greatly from the resultant continuity of personnel and policy.

Clinton and George W. Bush, by contrast, had no Washington experience, and both emphasized discontinuity with their predecessors. Many of their advisers felt even more strongly the need to do so. Most of these advisers had Washington experience, but it was dated, the world, in both cases, having changed dramatically while their parties were out of power. Clinton faltered immediately in Somalia. Bush did well at first in Afghanistan but did not sustain that success in Iraq, or, for that matter, in Afghanistan.

Frequent elections, the two-party system, and presidential term limits are designed to produce benefits that transcend technical competence in the design and implementation of foreign policy. Alternation in power is, in fact, an essential condition and necessary product of democracy. The 22nd Amendment of the Constitution, which set term limits for all future presidents and was passed in immediate aftermath of President Roosevelt's successful conduct of World War II, represents a rather explicit national choice for innovation over expertise.

In the U.S. case, however, the costs and risks associated with presidential transitions are magnified by the role of political patronage in staffing the national security establishment. The United States' reliance on the "spoils" system to empty and fill thousands of high- and medium-level policy positions every four, eight, or 12 years is unmatched in the Western world. The effect is to ensure a high degree of inexperience in the opening years of many presidencies, particularly when the opposition party comes to power. This reliance on patronage to fill key staff positions effectively insulates political leaders at the top from professional advice at the bottom, imposing several layers of ideological buffer between the two. It thus promotes barriers to continuity of policy from one administration to the next. It also results in diminished competence in a civil service whose members are denied access to positions of greater responsibility. These problems have become more acute in recent decades as the number of positions in the national security establishment subject to partisan selection has risen.

It is unrealistic to think that a country as large, varied, and dynamic as the United States could be administered by a civil service of elite mandarins on the basis of British, French, or German models. Nevertheless, Congress has largely walled off the U.S. military, law enforcement, and intelligence services from patronage appointments on the grounds that public security is too important to be politicized. Setting aside some proportion of subcabinet and White House staff positions in the national security arena for career personnel could be similarly justified and would go far to diminish the turbulence associated with changes in administrations, thereby reducing the alarming incidence of neophyte presidents making flawed decisions on the advice of loyal but inadequately experienced staff.

Acknowledgments

The authors would like to thank Vartan Gregorian and Steven Del Rosso of the Carnegie Corporation for their support of this study and David Rothkopf and Stuart Johnson for their thoughtful and constructive reviews.

Abbreviations

CIA	Central Intelligence Agency
CJTF 7	Combined Joint Task Force 7
CPA	Coalition Provisional Authority
DoD	U.S. Department of Defense
DOS	U.S. Department of State
ESG	Executive Steering Group (on Iraq)
EXCOM	executive committee
HR	high representative
HRG	National Security Council Humanitarian/ Reconstruction Group
IGC	Iraqi Governing Council
IFOR	NATO Implementation Force
IPA	international provisional administration
IPMC	National Security Council Iraq Political-Military Cell
ISAF	International Security Assistance Force (first under national command, then part of NATO)
IWG	interagency working group

JCS	Joint Chiefs of Staff
KFOR	NATO Kosovo Force
KLA	Kosovo Liberation Army
KVM	Kosovo Verification Mission
NATO	North Atlantic Treaty Organization
NGO	nongovernmental organization
NSC	National Security Council
NSC/DC	National Security Council Deputies Committee
NSC/PC	National Security Council Principals Committee
NSPD	National Security Presidential Directive
NSRD	National Security Research Division
OMGUS	Office of Military Government of the United States
OPLAN	operations plan
ORHA	Office of Reconstruction and Humanitarian Assistance
OSCE	Organization for Security and Co-Operation in Europe
OSP	U.S. Department of Defense Office of Special Plans
PDD	Presidential Decision Directive
PIC	Peace Implementation Council
PRD	Presidential Review Directive
PRT	provisional reconstruction team

PVO	private voluntary organization
SACEUR	Supreme High Commander Europe
SCAP	Supreme Commander of the Allied Powers
SFOR	NATO Stabilization Force
SHAEF	Supreme Headquarters Allied Expeditionary Force
SWNCC	State-War-Navy Coordinating Committee
UN	United Nations
UNAMA	United Nations Assistance Mission in Afghanistan
UNHCR	United Nations High Commissioner for Refugees
UNITAF	Unified Task Force
UNMIH	United Nations Mission in Haiti
UNMIK	United Nations Mission in Kosovo
UNOSOM	United Nations Operation in Somalia
UNSC	United Nations Security Council
USACOM	U.S. Atlantic Command
USAID	U.S. Agency for International Development
USCENTCOM	U.S. Central Command
USFET	U.S. Forces European Theater

CHAPTER ONE

Introduction

The United States has attempted at least eight significant nation-building operations over the past 60 years, beginning with the occupations of Germany and Japan at the conclusion of World War II. The next major spate of nation-building came at the end of the Cold War, in Somalia, Haiti, Bosnia, and Kosovo. Finally, in the aftermath of the September 11, 2001, attacks, the United States has found itself similarly involved in both Afghanistan and Iraq. The post–World War II operations were planned under Franklin D. Roosevelt and carried out under Harry Truman. The first post–Cold War operation was initiated by George H. W. Bush; it and three subsequent missions were conducted under William J. Clinton. Yet, perhaps, no president's foreign policy has been more dominated by nation-building than that of George W. Bush.

In all eight cases, the style, structure, and process of presidential decisionmaking have affected the mission's outcome. Administrations learned lessons from their own activities that they later applied to their operations. Unfortunately, there has been less carry-forward of expertise from one administration to the next. This monograph suggests remedies to that deficiency, examines how successive presidents and their national security teams have approached the initiation and management of nation-building operations, and identifies best practices for the conduct of such operations in the future.

Decisionmaking processes are central to the functioning of government. Without structure, decisions are often delayed, made without analysis, or simply not made at all. Further, even the best decisions can go unimplemented without a sound structure to task and coordinate the relevant federal agencies. This can occur even absent the infighting, personality clashes, and willful obstruction that are not uncommon in the executive branch.

Nation-building can be defined as the use of armed forces in the aftermath of a conflict to promote an enduring peace and a transition to democracy. Other terms currently in use to describe this process include *stabilization and reconstruction, peace-building, and state-building.* Since 1989, the frequency, duration, and scope of such missions have grown exponentially, with no end in sight, either for the United States or the rest of the international community.

Presidential style and bureaucratic structure are by no means the sole determinants of success in any such endeavor. In previous volumes, we have looked at the nature of the societies being reformed, the level of external resources applied to the process, and the content of the policies effected.[1] But if style, process, and structure are not dispositive, they do exert an important influence. Some of the previously mentioned administrations proved better at this task than did others. All improved over time, but those improvements have not always been passed on undiminished to their successors. This monograph looks at how successive presidents and their national security teams made and implemented decisions, and identifies barriers to the transmission of accrued expertise in the field of nation-building from one administration to the next.

---

[1]   See James Dobbins, John G. McGinn, Keith Crane, Seth G. Jones, Rollie Lal, Andrew Rathmell, Rachel M. Swanger, and Anga R. Timilsina, *America's Role in Nation-Building: From Germany to Iraq,* Santa Monica, Calif.: RAND Corporation, MR-1753-RC, 2003; James Dobbins, Seth G. Jones, Keith Crane, Andrew Rathmell, Brett Steele, Richard Teltschik, and Anga R. Timilsina, *The UN's Role in Nation-Building: From the Congo to Iraq,* Santa Monica, Calif.: RAND Corporation, MG-304-RC, 2005; and James Dobbins, Seth G. Jones, Keith Crane, and Beth Cole DeGrasse, *The Beginner's Guide to Nation-Building,* Santa Monica, Calif.: RAND Corporation, MG-557-SRF, 2007.

CHAPTER TWO

Presidential Style, Institutional Structure, and Bureaucratic Process

The president is both constitutionally and empirically the prime mover of U.S. foreign policy. Executive-branch decisionmaking structure and process has, accordingly, been subjected to considerable scrutiny. For the purposes of this study, two intellectual frameworks were particularly instructive: Graham Allison and Philip Zelikow's governmental politics model of decisionmaking and Alexander George's work on presidential decisionmaking.

In their revised edition of Allison's seminal work *Essence of Decision*, Allison and Zelikow argue against the "rational-actor" model of governmental decisionmaking, which posits that a unitary actor—in this case, the executive branch of the U.S. government—calculates the costs and benefits of a particular policy and chooses to implement a course of action that maximizes its strategic goals and objectives. According to this model, analysts can infer a presidential administration's references merely by rigorously examining the policy outcome. Process in decisionmaking is important only inasmuch as accurate information about the costs and benefits of the courses of action under consideration are made available to the decisionmakers—the president and presidential advisers—who are assumed to share a unity of purpose.[1]

However, as Allison and Zelikow point out, this academically pure model of decisionmaking bears little resemblance to the realities of everyday practice in the U.S. government. Knowledge of the presi-

---

[1] See Graham Allison and Philip Zelikow, *Essence of Decision: Explaining the Cuban Missile Crisis*, 2nd ed., New York: Longman, 1999, pp. 13–54.

dent's initial preferences is, by itself, rarely sufficient for explaining or predicting policy outcomes. Within a broad framework of shared values and interests, government officials frequently have competitive rather than identical operational objectives. "It is quite natural," Allison and Zelikow note, "that each feels special responsibility to call attention to the ramifications of an issue for his or her domain."[2] Often, these priorities are determined as much by the preferences of the governmental organizations they represent as by a neutral, rational cost-benefit analysis. Consequently, government behavior and policy outcomes are best understood as the result of bargaining and compromise among the various officials and advisers surrounding the president.

Cautioning that "policy outcomes result from multiple causes that defy simple summary and easily solution," Allison and Zelikow argue that the outcome of this process is determined by an array of variables including, but not limited to the following:

- Who plays? (Which officials and advisers will be taking part in any given decision?)
- What shapes the players' perceptions and preferences? (What are the personality traits, organizational goals, and interests to be advocated?)
- What determines each player's impact on results? (What are the bargaining advantages of formal authority or responsibility and control over resources or information?)

Moreover, the factors that provide an official with bargaining advantages in one "action channel" may not confer similar advantages in a different setting. The ability to frame the issue for decisionmaking (and, consequently, who gets to set the terms of the discussion) also has a significant impact on how the bargaining process will play out.[3]

The personal approach of individual presidents to decisionmaking is also critically important to the end results. In *Presidential Decisionmaking in Foreign Policy*, Alexander George presents three "ideal" pres-

---

[2] Allison and Zelikow (1999, pp. 256, 258).

[3] Allison and Zelikow (1999, pp. 263, 298, 300, 302).

idential approaches to decisionmaking, derived from earlier work by Richard Johnson: the formalistic, the competitive, and the collegial.[4]

The formalistic model is defined by a heavy reliance on hierarchy and staff analysis. In this model, lower-level analysis conducted within the executive branch and integrated through the National Security Council screens and "digests" information for senior policymakers. This process generates specific options that are presented to the president and cabinet-level advisers. This model attempts to downplay conflict through the extensive staff collaboration required, as many issues of contention will have either been resolved or simply incorporated as trade-offs in the various options generated.

The formalistic model has two principal advantages. The first is that a highly structured decisionmaking process tends to ensure that the issues are thoroughly analyzed. This helps to ensure that the president and senior advisers are made aware of all pros and cons of particular options. The second advantage is that it conserves the president's and senior advisers' time (always in short supply) by involving them principally in the selection, rather than the generation, of options.

The strength of this model is also a source of two weaknesses. The first is that such a hierarchic and analysis-intensive process requires quite a lot of time. Papers and memoranda must be prepared, working groups held, briefings given, and so forth. Among other things, this makes crisis response difficult. The second weakness is that the very process by which information is processed may distort the information and, therefore, the options presented to the president and senior advisers. For example, options may be ruled out as technically or economically infeasible early in the staffing process for reasons that are convincing to junior officials but would be less persuasive for senior officials, had they been given a chance to consider the matter. This model of decisionmaking is most associated with Presidents Dwight D. Eisenhower and Richard Nixon.[5]

---

[4] Alexander L. George, *Presidential Decisionmaking in Foreign Policy: The Effective Use of Information and Advice*, Boulder, Colo.: Westview Press, 1980, pp. 148–149; see also Richard Johnson, *Managing the White House*, New York: Harper and Row, 1974.

[5] George (1980, pp. 151–152).

The competitive model is, in many ways, the opposite of the formalistic. This model is associated with the creation of overlapping or ambiguous lines of authority among executive-branch agencies, limited communication between agencies and advisers, and a willingness of the president to listen to a wide array of opinions presented in an ad hoc fashion by competing advisers. In some cases, the president will also communicate directly with subordinates several levels of hierarchy lower in executive agencies, e.g., at the under secretary or assistant secretary levels.

This model has one central advantage, which is that competition among subordinates and agencies can spur superior performance and the generation of new ideas. In effect, decisionmaking is the result of a classic marketplace of ideas. Information will also be less distorted by the bureaucratic process if the president reaches several layers down into the bureaucracy while also cultivating outside advisers—the classic "kitchen cabinet" arrangement.[6]

However, this model has two drawbacks. The first is that it can place major demands on the president's time and intellect, as the president is the principal arbiter of the competition and the integrator of the result. The second is that competition among agencies and advisers can degenerate into outright hostility, leading to strained working relationships among key components of the executive branch and possibly resulting in the active sabotage of decisions after they are made. The archetypal example of this model, as discussed in more detail in the next chapter, is the Roosevelt administration's decisionmaking process.

The collegial model, as George notes, "attempts to achieve the essential advantages of each of the other two while avoiding their pitfalls."[7] This model encourages the free exchange of ideas, as in the competitive model, but seeks to foster a cooperative rather than competitive relationship among executive-branch agencies. Lateral communication among these agencies is valued nearly as highly as vertical communication within them (and to the president).

---

[6]   George (1980, pp. 149–150).

[7]   George (1980, p. 149).

This model, despite attempting to avoid the problems of the other two, has one problem of its own: The close and cooperative relationship among so many of the president's advisers and agencies is susceptible to what Irving Janis has termed *groupthink*. This condition is one in which ideas, once formulated by a tightly knit group, become so accepted that they become virtually unchangeable.[8] Without competition, there are simply no alternative sources of credible information outside the group. This model is most associated with the George H. W. Bush administration.

These three models provide a starting point for the examination and comparison of how presidents structure their decisionmaking processes. However, each president is unique, so the characteristics of an individual president are also critically important. In practice, each president's personality produces a decisionmaking structure that falls somewhere among the archetypes. Harry Truman, for example, was much more formalistic than was his predecessor, Roosevelt, but much less so than his successor, Eisenhower. George H. W. Bush fell somewhere between the formalistic and the collegial models, while Clinton was more a combination of competitive and collegial.

Whereas Allison and Zelikow emphasize bottom-up influences on the decisionmaking process, George identifies three parameters of presidential personality that affect how a president will structure decisionmaking. The first is cognitive style, which includes mental constructs about how the world works, how the individual prefers to receive information (e.g., written versus oral, formal briefing versus informal conversation), and how much information he or she needs about a subject before being willing to make a decision. The second is a sense of efficacy: an individual's competency in decisionmaking and management tasks. Some presidents, for example, feel very competent "in the weeds" of policy, while others feel less so. The third parameter is orientation toward conflict, both political and interpersonal. Presidents who

---

[8]   See, for example, Irving L. Janis, *Groupthink: Psychological Studies of Policy Decisions and Fiascos*, 2nd ed., Boston, Mass.: Houghton Mifflin, 1982, and Irving L. Janis and Leon Mann, *Decision Making: A Psychological Analysis of Conflict, Choice, and Commitment*, New York: Free Press, 1977.

are very comfortable with partisan politics and personal clashes tend to structure their decisionmaking process very differently from those who shy away from conflict of this sort.[9]

The personalities surrounding a president, both in cabinet-level agencies and among White House staff, also affect decisionmaking. Over time, considerable influence has shifted from the cabinet to the White House staff, but powerful cabinet secretaries can nonetheless have significant influence over decisionmaking. Secretary of Defense Robert McNamara, for example, held considerable sway in presidential decisionmaking concerning almost all aspects of national security—from the deployment of nuclear forces to the Vietnam War. Similarly, National Security Advisor Henry Kissinger and his National Security Council (NSC) staff also profoundly affected presidential decisionmaking.

The next three chapters present brief sketches of five presidents' administrative styles and personalities, characterizing them in terms of the three categories presented in this chapter. It is important to recognize, however, that the categories are archetypes that will seldom, if ever, conform to a given example. Most presidents not only apply some hybrid or mix of elements of the categories, but they change these mixes over time. Roosevelt is perhaps the closest to an ideal type relative to the others examined, and he varied in his style with time and circumstance.

Second, regardless of efficacy, a president's style is largely dependent on the individual. This limits the amount of freedom to design an "optimal" decisionmaking structure for nation-building, as this structure will vary from president to president. George concludes that there is no silver bullet to ensure better policymaking decisions, noting, "In brief, the present emphasis is on designing organizational structures to fit the operating styles of their key individuals rather than attempting to persuade each new top executive to accept and adapt to a standardized organizational model that is considered to be theoretically

---

[9]   George (1980, pp. 147–148).

the best."[10] A one-size-fits-all, generic structure for nation-building will likely fail to conform to the needs of a given president and will thus be suboptimal. On the other hand, as this examination shows, excessive innovation in structure and process to suit individual presidential preference comes at a high cost in terms of continuity of expertise and quality of government performance.

As Allison and Zelikow note, "[M]aking sure the government does what is decided is more difficult than selecting the preferred solution."[11] The bargaining process and organizational competition for influence on policy outcomes does not stop once the president has signed off on a decision. Rather,

> most decisions leave considerable leeway in implementation. Players who support the decision maneuver to see it implemented, often going beyond the spirit and sometimes even the letter of the decision. Those who oppose the decision, or oppose the action, maneuver to delay implementation, to limit implementation, to raise the issue again with a different face or in another channel.[12]

Consequently, the implementation of decisions may frequently produce outcomes not foreseeable by a model of decisionmaking that emphasizes presidential personality.

---

[10] Alexander L. George and Eric Stern, "Presidential Management Styles and Models," in Alexander L. George and Juliette L. George, eds., *Presidential Personality and Performance*, Boulder, Colo.: Westview Press, 1998, pp. 200–201.

[11] Allison and Zelikow (1999, p. 258).

[12] Allison and Zelikow (1999, p. 304).

CHAPTER THREE

Post–World War II Nation-Building: Germany and Japan

The transformation of Nazi Germany and imperial Japan into peaceful, prosperous, vibrant democracies remains to this day the gold standard of nation-building. However, if, prior to 1945, one were to have characterized the United States' postwar plans for Germany and Japan as *nation-building*, the American public and many key U.S. decisionmakers would have responded with alarm. Faced with the practical problems of governing and feeding millions of Germans and Japanese, and with the threat of further Soviet expansion, U.S. policy shifted over time away from harshly punitive measures and toward the reform, reconstruction, and reintegration of these societies into the Western community. While these factors can explain the evolution of U.S. policy, they do not account for its success. To understand that, it is necessary to examine the structure and processes in President Roosevelt's administration; postwar planning efforts at the U.S. Department of State (DOS), the Department of War, and the Department of the Treasury and the interagency structures that brought those efforts together; the role of allied summits and coordinating agencies in the postwar planning; the implementation of postwar plans through U.S. military governance in both Germany and Japan, including the flow of information from the theater to Washington and subsequent direction from Washington to the theater; and the transition from occupation to the integration of Germany and Japan into the international establishment.

The Presidents and Their Administrations

Roosevelt served at the head of the first modern presidential bureaucracy, but the last presidency to lack a standing interagency organization for dealing with problems of national security. Roosevelt was, above all, a politician, and when choosing his cabinet, he looked for individuals who would not overshadow him or threaten him politically. Roosevelt's selections for under secretaries and assistant secretaries, however, were generally of excellent quality, and he frequently circumvented his cabinet members to directly task or take advice from these more junior officials. His personal leadership drove broad government efforts coordinated across various agencies. Roosevelt created a competitive environment in his administration.

> "A little rivalry is stimulating, you know. . . . It keeps everybody going to prove he is a better fellow than the next man. It keeps them honest too." In practice, the balancing of opposites sharpened internal policy debates, but the price paid was that frictions often carried over into program implementation.[1]

Roosevelt was a gifted, charismatic leader, able to keep a multitude of opposing ideas in his head. That ability, coupled with the competitive environment he had created, allowed Roosevelt to maintain tight control over his administration, despite the absence of a large White House staff. In addition to maneuvering around cabinet members or intentionally putting them at odds with one another,

> Roosevelt had little respect for jurisdictional boundaries. Secretary of the Treasury [Henry] Morgenthau was given assignments that rightly belonged to Secretary of State [Cordell] Hull and Secretary of War Harry Woodring. Cabinet members survived as best they could in this laissez-faire atmosphere, if not by implicit contract with their fellow department heads, then by conquest.[2]

---

[1] Stephen Hess and James P. Pfiffner, *Organizing the Presidency*, 3rd ed., Washington, D.C.: Brookings Institution Press, 2002, p. 24.

[2] Hess and Pfiffner (2002, p. 29); George (1980, pp. 149–150).

Roosevelt could thus be characterized as having a very open, free-flowing cognitive style, a strong and well-justified sense of his own efficacy in management, a mastery of policy details, and a very high level of comfort with conflict.

Through most of the war, although he allowed occupation planning to go forward, Roosevelt did not want to spend his time on the subject. First, he felt that winning the war was more urgent than planning for the peace. Second, he felt that any planning for the occupation would have to be changed, because it would not reflect the realities that would exist at the end of hostilities. Roosevelt told Hull, his Secretary of State, "I dislike making detailed plans for a country we do not yet occupy."[3] Finally, by deferring any decisions on the occupation, he was able to "keep the ultimate power of decision in his own hands."[4]

Unfortunately, when he became interested in planning for the occupation in 1944, his failing health had begun to have a significant impact on his ability to do so. "He no longer had the patience and command of detail that had once let him keep important policies from going off the rails and Cabinet members from exceeding the roles he envisaged for them."[5] In late March 1945, Secretary of War Henry Stimson described the President's "indecision" on postwar Germany in his personal writings: "Never has anything which I have witnessed in the last four years shown such instance of the bad effect of our chaotic administration and its utter failure to treat matters in a well-organized way."[6] Despite Roosevelt's desire throughout much of the war to defer occupation planning, officials in DOS, the Department of War, and the Department of the Treasury knew that advanced planning was necessary. The United States could not wait until Germany or Japan was in allied hands before deciding what their future would be and how it would be achieved. Unfortunately, that plan-

---

[3] Michael Beschloss, *The Conquerors: Roosevelt, Truman and the Destruction of Hitler's Germany, 1941–1945*, New York: Simon and Schuster, 2002, p. 159.

[4] Beschloss (2002, p. 19).

[5] Beschloss (2002, p. 84).

[6] Beschloss (2002, p. 200).

ning would be done with little policy direction from the top, of which much would be vague and inconsistent.

Following Roosevelt's death, it would fall to the administration of President Harry Truman to actually execute nation-building in Germany and Japan. Stylistically, Truman was almost the opposite of Roosevelt. Stephen Hess notes, "Harry S. Truman, a tidy man himself, was offended by Roosevelt's freewheeling style as an administrator."[7]

Truman instituted a much more formal model of presidential decisionmaking, though not as formal as that of his successor, Eisenhower. He was much more willing to take personal responsibility for potentially unpopular decisions, famously claiming of his Oval Office desk, "The buck stops here." He was much less comfortable with the type of political contestation for which Roosevelt was known, and he also introduced more collegial elements.

Truman himself had minimal executive-brand experience, having spent his career in Missouri politics and in the U.S. Senate. He compensated for this by bringing on several highly effective assistants, including the young Clark Clifford, who would later be Robert McNamara's successor as Secretary of Defense. Truman's cabinet was a mix of old political allies from Missouri and highly effective administrators. He also had a stable of tremendously experienced military leaders from whom to draw: Douglas McArthur, who governed Japan; Dwight D. Eisenhower, who became Army Chief of Staff and later commanded U.S. and North Atlantic Treaty Organization (NATO) forces in Europe; Omar Bradley, who succeeded Eisenhower as Chief of Staff and later became the first Chair of the Joint Chiefs of Staff; Walter Bedell Smith, who headed the Central Intelligence Agency (CIA); and George Marshall, who became Secretary of State. Overall, Truman can be characterized as having a methodical cognitive style, a sense of his own efficacy as a manager and final decisionmaker (rather than as a creator of detailed policies) and an aversion to high levels of conflict.

---

[7]   Hess and Pfiffner (2002, p. 36).

Planning for the Postwar Period

Between 1942 and 1944, DOS, the Department of War, and the Department of the Treasury each undertook significant and largely independent postwar planning efforts. However, these efforts were plagued by unanswered questions. Would it be a "hard" or "soft" peace? Everyone agreed that mistakes were made in the wake of the First World War that had led to the second, and "never again" was a mantra. However, it was unclear exactly what *never again* meant. Was the mistake in punishing Germany too harshly, or had it not been punished enough? Would Germany and Japan become the centerpieces of regional and economic stability, or would they be broken so badly that it would take decades for them to recover? Would Germany and Japan be needed as buffers between the West and an expansionist Soviet Union after the war? Some guidance was provided to the planners in announcements after international summit meetings, as when Roosevelt and Winston Churchill announced the goal of unconditional surrender after the Casablanca Conference in January 1943. But for the most part, each group of planners worked with limited guidance.

Roosevelt tasked DOS with postwar planning in late 1941, and one of his personal friends, Under Secretary of State Sumner Welles, led the initial effort. Welles had been working on postwar planning since 1939, initially focusing on plans for an international organization that would become the United Nations (UN). In early 1942, he formed a postwar planning committee. Welles involved individuals from many agencies and organizations inside and outside the U.S. government, including representatives of the Division of Special Research in DOS, Roosevelt's staff, the Board of Economic Warfare, the Department of Agriculture, the Council on Foreign Relations, U.S. Steel, and the *New York Times*. He also included key Democrats and Republicans from the House and Senate, as well as Isaiah Bowman, who had earlier served on President Woodrow Wilson's inquiry into postwar issues after World War I. Welles's postwar planning committee was comprised of five subcommittees: political problems, security problems, economic reconstruction, economic policy, and territorial problems. The subcommittees met and reported weekly from January 1942 until the committee was disbanded in July 1943, developing U.S. policy options in a multitude of areas regarding postwar Germany and Japan.

Members of Welles's committee assumed a soft position on Germany, believing that Germany would play a critical role in both the reconstruction of Europe and the new world order. They believed that the harsh punishment meted out at Versailles was a contributing factor that led to World War II and wanted to avoid repeating such mistakes. The group agreed on the demand for unconditional surrender, occupation by allied forces, and permanent disarmament. They believed that the punishment of war criminals, denazification, and reeducation of the German people would be critical in the rehabilitation and reintegration of Germany into Europe. The planning group felt that war reparations would create instability in Germany and encourage resentment and therefore should be avoided. They were concerned that the mass movement of refugees in the wake of the war could result in economic chaos or collapse. The one subject on which the group could not agree was whether to partition Germany. Either a strong, unified Germany or a weak, impoverished Germany would be dangerous for the future of Europe. There were recommendations to place German industry and transportation under international control, as well as to partition Germany into any number of smaller states. Even as early as 1942, planners understood that a stable Germany could help prevent Soviet expansion across Europe. Welles eventually proposed forming a loose German federation of three states with limited, central control measures that would allow the country's integration into the greater European economy. [8]

The recommendations for Japan were similar in many respects. The committee prepared position papers on six topics: occupational government, disarmament, internal political problems, disposition of Japanese territory, economic issues, and Japan's role in regional and international security organizations.[9] Welles saw the importance of

---

[8]   Christopher D. O'Sullivan, *Sumner Welles, Postwar Planning, and the Quest for a New World Order, 1937–1943*, New York: Columbia University Press, 2003, Chapter 5.

[9]   Marlene J. Mayo, "American Wartime Planning for Occupied Japan: The Role of the Experts," in Robert Wolfe, ed., *Americans as Proconsuls: United States Military Government in*

strong commercial ties with Japan. The committee called for unconditional surrender and for Japan to be stripped of most of its empire, occupied by allied troops, and demilitarized. Japan would then be integrated into the world economy, and its economic viability would be guaranteed through free trade. The committee could not resolve the relative importance of China versus Japan to U.S. interests in the Far East. The future of China as a great power was also an element of dispute among the allies, with the United States advocating for a strong China. Aside from the recommendation for unconditional surrender, it does not appear that the efforts of Welles's postwar planning committee had any immediate impact on presidential decisionmaking before it was disbanded by Secretary of State Cordell Hull in July 1943 in the wake of Welles's resignation.

On October 20, 1943, DOS created the Interdivisional Area Committee on the Far East to coordinate and develop policy for the occupation of Japan. Losing the interagency composition that Welles had created in his committee, this committee was comprised of "Japan hands" from the DOS Territorial Studies Division and the Division of Far Eastern Affairs, as well as expert economists, political scientists, and lawyers. It met 221 times between its formation and July 1945. A similar organization was created for German postwar planning, and both fed position papers to the DOS Postwar Programs Committee. By late 1944, these papers had become DOS policy and were used to answer planning questions from both the Department of War and the Navy.[10]

War Department planning for the postwar period began in earnest when the Civil Affairs Division was established under the leadership of Major General John H. Hilldring on May 4, 1943. As head of the division, Hilldring served on General George C. Marshall's special staff and was responsible for "planning the nonmilitary aspects of

Germany and Japan, 1944–1952, Carbondale, Ill.: Southern Illinois University Press, 1984, p. 16.

[10] Mayo (1984, pp. 23–24, 28–29).

whatever occupations the Army would have to handle in the future."[11] By the time the Civil Affairs Division was created, there were two other military organizations working on postwar issues. One was the Joint Post-War Committee of the Joint Chiefs of Staff, which focused only on drafting surrender documents. The other was the Military Government Division, which had three responsibilities: publishing civil affairs handbooks, operating military government training schools, and providing staging areas for Military Government Division officers prior to their assumption of duties in occupied areas.

The Military Government Division had been created in January 1942 in the Army's Office of the Provost Marshall, and through the training schools, they had worked on some of the issues that Hilldring would face. But the training school at the University of Virginia became a political liability, drawing the ire of the President soon after its creation. The Civil Affairs Division had been established separately, in part because of these political issues, and Hilldring did not want to be tainted by association with the Military Government Division. Next, Hilldring looked to see the current state of planning in DOS, but he found that "State, steeped in its traditional view of diplomacy and foreign policy, shunned anything that smacked of operations. . . . The gap between State's grand policies and the concrete tasks of Hilldring's organization was too wide."[12]

Hilldring next looked to newer civilian war agencies that had been created by Roosevelt, including the Foreign Economic Administration, the Office of Strategic Services, the Office of War Information, and the Economic Institutions Staff (initially within the Bureau of Economic Warfare but eventually moved to Foreign Economic Administration). To harness expertise across such disparate agencies, Hilldring commissioned the creation of more than 70 civil affairs guides on various issues related to the occupation of Germany and Japan. Among other agencies, the Economic Institutions Staff agreed to prepare 22 guides, the Office of Strategic Services agreed to prepare 25, the Civil Affairs Divi-

---

[11] Theodore Cohen, *Remaking Japan: The American Occupation as New Deal*, Herbert Passin, ed., New York: Free Press, 1987, p. 15.

[12] Cohen (1987, p. 21).

sion itself took on three guides, and the Department of Agriculture prepared one. Next, to get higher-level consensus on major issues, Hilldring established the Committee on Civil Affairs Studies and invited DOS, War, Navy, Treasury, Strategic Services, Agriculture, and the Foreign Economic Administration to participate, with the plan that the committee's working groups would review the newly drafted civil affairs guides. Many working on the guides for Japanese policy, "new to Washington, wondered whether this was not the way the Government normally operated—in a fog," and joked among themselves that, "if the war were suddenly to end, top officials, in a rush and for want of anything else, might just scoop our memos off our desks and declare them United States policy after all."[13]

In August 1944, while traveling to Europe under the guise of studying currency problems in newly liberated France, Harry Dexter White, the chief international economist at the Treasury Department, gave Secretary of the Treasury Henry Morgenthau a DOS memo on policy for postwar Germany. Morgenthau believed in collective guilt, feeling that Germany should be punished for the war and that the reparations on Germany after World War I had not gone far enough. White knew that the DOS memo, which was soft on Germany, would enrage Morgenthau.

Later, while in England, Colonel Bernard Bernstein, a member of Eisenhower's staff and previously a lawyer at the Treasury Department, provided Morgenthau with a copy of the draft *Handbook for Military Government in Germany*. The German Country Unit, a section of military government planners working in Eisenhower's Supreme Headquarters Allied Expeditionary Force (SHAEF), had prepared the handbook. The handbook was also soft on Germany, calling for the restoration of the German civilian government as soon as possible during the occupation. This idea, while reasonable from a military government perspective, with its limited staffing and strategy for a short occupation, was the opposite of what Morgenthau expected.[14] While in London, Morgenthau also met with John Winant, U.S. ambassador to Great

---

[13] Cohen (1987, pp. 24–26).

[14] Beschloss (2002, pp. 70–71).

Britain, who told him that "he had tried for months to get instructions from Washington. But he had no idea what Roosevelt wanted to do about postwar Germany."[15] Immediately upon his return to Washington, Morgenthau took his copy of the handbook to Roosevelt, who reviewed it. Roosevelt provided his opinion in a memo to Secretary of War Stimson: "This so-called *Handbook* is pretty bad. . . . It gives me the impression that Germany is to be restored just as much as the Netherlands or Belgium."[16] Stimson had told Roosevelt earlier that day "that American troops were about to enter Germany with 'no instructions' or 'vital points.'"[17]

Morgenthau, unhappy with the direction in which U.S. planning was headed and feeling that it did not reflect the desires of the President, a long-time personal friend and neighbor in New York, took it upon himself to take the lead on postwar planning for Germany. In early September 1944, Harry Dexter White and a small team at the Treasury Department drafted what would become known as the Morgenthau Plan, though its formal title was the *Program to Prevent Germany from Starting a World War III*.[18] The plan included such measures as destroying all German heavy industry; giving German equipment, labor, and other resources to victims of Nazi aggression, with the bulk going to the Soviet Union; and shooting Nazi war criminals without trial. For two weeks, Morgenthau's plan was bitterly debated at the newly formed Cabinet Committee on Germany made up of Stimson, Hull, and Morgenthau, with one of Roosevelt's closest advisers, Harry Hopkins, presiding. At the end of the first meeting, Stimson said that the committee was "irreconcilably divided," and Hull said, "If anybody has a plan, let him send it separately."[19] When meeting with the committee, Roosevelt played each man off the other, appearing to agree with one position on one day and another the next. With no agree-

---

[15] Beschloss (2002, p. 77).

[16] Beschloss (2002, p. 95).

[17] Beschloss (2002, p. 94).

[18] Beschloss (2002, p. 115).

[19] Beschloss (2002, p. 106).

ment among the committee members on postwar plans for Germany, Roosevelt left for the Quebec Conference in mid-September 1944.

Although Roosevelt had invited Hull to join him in Quebec, Hull declined, explaining that he was too tired. Once Roosevelt arrived at the conference, he sent for Morgenthau, later telling Interior Secretary Harold Ickes that "he summoned Morgenthau because he had 'the only definite information' on Germany 'that anyone seemed to have.'"[20] At the Quebec Conference, Morgenthau briefed British Prime Minister Winston Churchill on his plan for postwar Germany. Churchill was initially angered by the proposal, stating that "he would not chain himself to a 'dead German.'"[21] However, over the course of the conference, Roosevelt persuaded Churchill to agree to Morgenthau's plan. Soon after Quebec, details of the plan were leaked to the *Wall Street Journal*, likely by the War Department, resulting in a propaganda coup for Germany. General Marshall complained to Morgenthau that publicity of his plan was increasing German resistance. Soon, the *New York Times* was reporting that Roosevelt had changed his mind on the Morgenthau Plan, and the President abolished the Cabinet Committee on Germany. The committee had met for only one month, and Morgenthau's plan was abandoned, but its effect would be lasting.

Members of DOS felt that Morgenthau had exploited his friendship with Roosevelt in pushing his plan forward, but he had been initially successful because of "the absence of a mechanism for political-military decisions through which all agencies had to go."[22] In November, the three secretaries involved established the State-War-Navy Coordinating Committee (SWNCC), a body to broadly address all political-military matters. Among other issues, the SWNCC and its subcommittees worked on plans for the occupation of Germany and Japan. While they had been successful in excluding Morgenthau, Hilldring's staff at the Civil Affairs Division had begun an early draft

---

[20] Beschloss (2002, p. 140).

[21] Beschloss (2002, p. 125).

[22] Cohen (1987, p. 33).

of what would become Joint Chiefs of Staff (JCS) Directive 1067,[23] the directive to General Eisenhower on the German occupation. They had written the draft while the Morgenthau Plan was understood to be U.S. policy, with Harry Dexter White frequently visiting the Civil Affairs Division to assist. Because nothing replaced the Morgenthau plan once it had been disavowed, the final version of JCS 1067 contained many of the harsh measures and all the intent of a hard peace toward Germany.

Having not given up on influencing postwar plans for Germany, Morgenthau convinced Roosevelt in March 1945 to form an interim policy committee on Germany that would include Treasury Department representation.[24] Thus, as the war was rapidly approaching its conclusion and policy organizations finally settled in Washington, the committee took on the job of planning for the occupation of Germany, and the SWNCC set up a subcommittee on the Far East that took on planning for the occupation of Japan. Morgenthau and his Treasury Department team showed little interest in planning for Japan's occupation; many of the plans that were developed for Germany were copied, in some cases word for word, in the plans for Japan. Consequently, Morgenthau's influence was felt in much of the planning for Japan as well.[25]

The eventual outputs of these two planning efforts were JCS 1067, SWNCC 150,[26] and JCS 1380.[27] The two JCS directives, in effect, took the policy guidance prepared by the Informal Policy Committee on Germany and the SWNCC and translated them into militarily execut-

---

[23] Joint Chiefs of Staff Directive 1067, Directive to Commander-in-Chief of United States Forces of Occupation Regarding the Military Government in Germany, April 1945.

[24] Hugh Borton, "Presuppositions, Prejudices, and Planning," in Robert Wolfe, ed., *Americans as Proconsuls: United States Military Government in Germany and Japan, 1944–1952*, Carbondale, Ill.: Southern Illinois University Press, 1984, p. 2.

[25] Cohen (1987, pp. 29–30).

[26] State-War-Navy Coordinating Committee Directive 150, Politico-Military Problems in the Far East: United States Initial Post-Defeat Policy Relating to Japan, September 1945.

[27] Joint Chiefs of Staff Directive 1380, Basic Directive for Post-Surrender Military Government in Japan Proper, November 1945.

able orders with significantly more operational details. Hilldring's civil affairs guides became useful in filling in those details. JCS 1067 was approved by President Truman in April 1945, but it could not be given to SHAEF as a directive because SHAEF was still a combined British and American headquarters, and JCS 1067 was a U.S. document. Thus, the directive would have to go through the allied organization in London before it could be implemented. Instead, this one was held "in abeyance" to be used by Eisenhower in his capacity as U.S. commander in the U.S. zone after the combined headquarters was dissolved.[28]

When Lieutenant General Lucius Clay arrived in Europe in May 1945 as the newly appointed deputy military governor, he had not yet seen JCS 1067. After he read it, he told Hilldring that "Washington apparently did not have clear idea of what conditions were like in Germany and asked to have the directive revised to make it 'flexible and general.'" Hilldring responded that it was better to have something than nothing and that it had been cleverly drafted by Stimson and his deputy McCloy to include loopholes:[29]

> This directive sets forth policies relating to Germany in the initial post-defeat period. As such it is not intended to be an ultimate statement of policies of this Government concerning the treatment of Germany in the postwar world. It is therefore essential that, during the period covered by this directive, you assure that surveys are constantly maintained of economic, industrial, financial, social and political conditions in your zone. . . . These surveys should be developed in such manner as to serve as a basis for determining changes in the measures of control set forth herein as well as for the progressive formulation and development of policies to promote the basic objectives of the United States.[30]

---

[28] Earl F. Ziemke, "Improvising Stability and Change in Postwar Germany," in Robert Wolfe, ed., *Americans as Proconsuls: United States Military Government in Germany and Japan, 1944–1952*, Carbondale, Ill.: Southern Illinois University Press, 1984, p. 58.

[29] Ziemke (1984, p. 58).

[30] Joint Chiefs of Staff Directive 1067 (1945).

Similarly, Supreme Commander of the Allied Powers (SCAP) General Douglas MacArthur arrived in Japan having not seen the directive that would govern his actions as the military governor of occupied Japan, as it had not yet been approved by the President. He was given a draft of SWNCC 150 when he arrived in Japan on August 30, 1945, and three weeks later, he received the first half of JCS 1380, governing the general and political facets of the occupation. It was not until October 22 that he received the entire directive, which included economic and financial specifications. While General Clay took great liberties in interpreting and implementing JCS 1067, General MacArthur directed his staff to execute JCS 1380 as it was written, accepting it as his own plan. No one in Japan would have believed that MacArthur himself had not written JCS 1380.

The Allies

Not surprisingly, allied views were much more important in defining the course of Germany's occupation than Japan's. In both cases, however, U.S. policy was ultimately decisive regarding all but Soviet-occupied eastern Germany.

During World War II and in its immediate aftermath, allied leaders met seven times to coordinate policy on the war and the peace that would follow. The first summit, between Roosevelt and Churchill in August 1941, was held off the coast of Newfoundland and resulted in the Atlantic Charter. The charter declared the purpose of the war and the nature of the world that would follow it. The charter was joined by 15 nations in September 1941. The next summit, in Casablanca in January 1943, also included only Roosevelt and Churchill. Stalin was invited but was occupied with the German offensive into the Soviet Union. At the end of the summit, Roosevelt told reporters that they had decided "that peace can come to the world only by the total elimination of German and Japanese war power," requiring "unconditional surrender by Germany, Italy, and Japan."[31] Stalin was angered by the

---

[31] Beschloss (2002, p. 14).

declaration. First, he had not been consulted. Second, he wanted a second front opened against Germany, not a declaration. Finally, he thought that such a declaration would harden German resolve and make winning the war more difficult.

The next meeting was held in Cairo in November 1943. This meeting, between Roosevelt, Churchill, and Chinese leader Chiang Kai-Shek, resulted in the Cairo Declaration. The three allies had reiterated the unconditional-surrender formula for Japan, called for Japan to be stripped of territorial gains made since the beginning of World War I, and expressed the desire that Korea become free and independent.[32] Immediately following the meeting in Cairo, the first summit between Roosevelt, Churchill, and Stalin was held in Tehran. At this meeting, they agreed to jointly try war criminals whose alleged crimes had taken place in more than one country. They also agreed, in general terms, that Germany should be partitioned into three occupation zones, one each for the United States, Great Britain, and the Soviet Union. They could not agree on the boundaries of the zones and directed the formation of the European Advisory Committee to make recommendations. This group first met on January 14, 1944, in London and was comprised of U.S. Ambassador John Winant, Sir William Strang for the British, and Ambassador F. T. Gusev for the Soviet Union. "Winant later frankly told Roosevelt by cable that in all 'recorded history,' he did not think that any 'commission created by governments for a serious purpose has had less support from the governments creating it than the European Advisory Commission.'"[33]

In September 1944, Churchill and Roosevelt met in Quebec, agreeing—for a short time—on Morgenthau's plan. The second, and last, meeting of Roosevelt, Churchill, and Stalin occurred at Yalta in February 1945. Despite Winant's description of the European Advisory Committee, at Yalta, the allies approved the only three documents that it had developed, providing for four separate zones of occupation in Germany, almost absolute authority for each of the military governors in these zones, and the joint administration of Berlin. While the

---

[32] Cairo Communiqué, December 1, 1943.

[33] Beschloss (2002, p. 30).

French were excluded from Yalta, it was at the summit that the boundaries of the French zone were determined; it was carved out of what had previously been the UK and U.S. zones.[34] The subsequent Yalta communiqué "publicly proclaimed that unconditional surrender and military occupation of Germany required disarmament, punishment of war criminals, eradication of Nazism, and payment of reparations."[35]

At Potsdam in July 1945, President Truman met with Stalin and, initially, Churchill, who was replaced during the summit by Clement Attlee. At Potsdam, the allies created the Allied Control Council, which would work in Berlin on issues that applied to Germany as a whole. They also agreed on the definition of German borders and war reparations. At Potsdam, Truman and Attlee also discussed the conditions to end the war with Japan. They stated that,

> while there would be no enslavement or destruction of the nation, there would be a period of occupation and military government, punishment of war criminals, loss of empire, elimination of militarism, economic disarmament, removal of obstacles to democratic tendencies, and the establishment of fundamental human rights.[36]

What was notably *not* required was the removal of the emperor. While many issues were discussed at allied summits throughout the war, Roosevelt kept most of the discussions to himself, refusing to share details with members of his cabinet. The only information with which they had to plan was what was released to the public in the various declarations and communiqués.

Several allied control structures were developed for the occupation. In Germany, the U.S. military governor reigned supreme in the U.S. zone, but for any issues outside the zone, he was forced to act through the Allied Control Council in Berlin. It quickly became clear

---

[34] Harold Zink, *The United States in Germany 1944–1955*, Princeton, N.J.: D. Van Nostrand Company, 1957, p. 23.

[35] Mayo (1984, p. 10).

[36] Mayo (1984, p. 44).

to Eisenhower and Clay, his deputy and later his successor as military governor, that little could be agreed on at the council. In late 1946, Clay and the British zone commander formed Bizonia, an economic merger of the U.S. and British zones, with its capital in Frankfurt, to improve economic recovery. Later, the French zone was included, and the three zones transitioned to a common currency. In response, the Soviets walked out of the Allied Control Commission and closed Berlin to western access, occasioning the Berlin airlift.[37] The de facto split between east and west in Germany began to crystallize.

Whereas Germany had been split into four zones, Japan remained whole during the occupation, with General Douglas MacArthur as the supreme authority in the country. The 11-nation Far Eastern Commission was established in Washington and the four-member Allied Council was established in Tokyo, but they had no appreciable influence on the occupation. A Far Eastern Commission decision that had never been acknowledged by the SCAP indicated that the "War Department officials involved had decided not to irritate the Supreme Commander by forwarding him a decision he might not like."[38] When the Allied Council in Tokyo met for the first time in April 1946, MacArthur, as the chair and U.S. representative, said a few words to open the session, designated U.S. Ambassador to Japan William J. Sebald his deputy on the council, and never attended another meeting.[39]

Implementation

The implementation of JCS 1067 and JCS 1380, the orders to Eisenhower and MacArthur laying out their instructions for the occupation of Germany and Japan, reflected the very different circumstances on the ground in the two countries. In Germany, military government units took over administration of German territory as a carpet unroll-

---

[37] Beschloss (2002, p. 279).

[38] Cohen (1987, p. 74).

[39] Charles A. Willoughby and John Chamberlain, *MacArthur 1941–1951*, New York: McGraw-Hill, 1954, p. 317.

ing in the wake of the advancing combat troops. Smaller detachments would be responsible for small towns and cities, and larger, more senior detachments would supervise them and be responsible for the German government at the state level. But that carpet, which began unrolling on September 15, 1944, quickly became very thin. By March, more than 150 military government detachments were deployed in Germany. In many small towns, officers merely posted occupation notices and moved on to the next town. These officers were supposed to control German government officials, not govern, but in many cases, there were no officials or any standing government buildings or services. Denazification policies meant that some Germans with the ability and experience to govern were removed.

In Japan, in contrast, the occupation of the homeland was effected after the surrender. In a short period, hundreds of thousands of U.S. troops spread across the islands. Chaos was avoided because the Japanese government remained largely intact. Where denazification in Germany had removed 2.5 percent of the population of the U.S. zone from any work but manual labor, in Japan, only 0.29 percent were purged over a two-year period, and of those, 80 percent were military officers.[40] In both cases, the U.S. military wanted to govern through the occupied nation's government. Only in Japan was that possible. In Japan, military government detachments were sent outside Tokyo. MacArthur's wartime headquarters staff took up residence in Tokyo to manage the occupation. Soon, experts in such areas as agriculture reform and economics joined the staff to manage the "shadow" government. MacArthur's Tokyo records describe the system:

> Since the Japanese civil government was capable of operating, Occupation authorities were relieved from directly administering a "conquered" country; instead, they were charged with seeing that the Japanese government complied with SCAP's directives. Military Government was also to advise Japanese officials on matters in which they had no previous experience under a totalitarian regime. In effect, there was no "military government" in Japan in

---

[40] Howard B. Schonberger, *Aftermath of War: Americans and the Remaking of Japan, 1945–1952*, Kent, Ohio: Kent State University Press, 1989.

the literal sense of the word. It was simply a SCAP superstructure over already existing government machinery, designed to observe and assist the Japanese along the new democratic channels of administration.[41]

The pace of implementation was different in Germany and Japan. While the German occupation was accused of foot-dragging, from the beginning in Japan, orders flowed quickly from the SCAP. In Germany, the allied military forces had to be redistributed from the areas that they had taken during combat operations and the zones that had been agreed upon at Yalta; it took nearly two months before the redistribution was completed and SHAEF, the combined command, was dissolved and replaced by U.S. Forces European Theater (USFET) and comparable British and French commands. The occupation in Japan did not have the same level of chaos and was able to make faster progress. In fact, MacArthur was moving so quickly that he got ahead of Washington at one point, announcing on September 17, 1945, that, since the Japanese government had been so helpful to the occupation, the U.S. military could reduce its presence from 500,000 to 200,000 troops in less than six months. Unfortunately, MacArthur had not cleared his estimate with anyone in Washington, and the JCS, DOS, and the White House were angry. All future comments on troop reductions had to be cleared through Washington.[42]

One consistent feature of the two occupations was the commanders' desire for quick elections that would start the citizens on the road toward democracy. In much of the political planning for the occupation, it was believed that it would take a generation or two for democracy to take hold in Germany and Japan. Certainly, the planners thought that democratic education would be necessary to teach the citizens how the system would work and about their role within it. The military commanders, wanting the occupation to be as short as possible, would not wait for a new education system or the passing of a generation. Clay's desire to hold elections so soon alarmed both

---

[41] Willoughby and Chamberlain (1954, pp. 307–309).

[42] Schonberger (1989, p. 48).

German politicians and his own advisers.[43] On September 20, 1945, he ordered the German state governments to write election codes and the military district commanders to prepare for elections in January 1946 for cities with populations below 20,000. Clay wrote to Assistant Secretary of War John McCloy, "If the Germans are to learn democracy, I think the best way is to start off quickly at the bottom."[44] In Japan, the SCAP moved forward quickly as well, and the first general election was held in April 1946.[45]

In Germany, the occupation had a strict nonfraternization policy. There had been numerous stories in the U.S. press that senior German prisoners of war had received friendly treatment, and, consequently, the American public was outraged. In response, on June 19, 1945, Eisenhower announced at a Washington press conference "that there could be no fraternization in Germany until the last Nazi criminals had been uprooted."[46] The soldiers on the ground in Germany, however, saw the Army's nonfraternization policy as punishment directed toward them. For most soldiers, the only Germans with whom they wanted to "fraternize" were women. A member of SHAEF headquarters noted that the Germans "could hardly fail to notice that something had gone wrong 'when large signs [reading] "Don't Fraternize" have to be displayed every 50 yards or so.'" The soldiers joked that they were giving the Germans the opportunity "to see Americans engaged in the most widespread violation of their own laws since Prohibition."[47] In contrast, in Japan, MacArthur told an aide,

> "I wouldn't issue a non-fraternization order for all the tea in China." He was convinced of the beneficial effect of greater con-

---

[43] John Gimbel, "Governing the American Zone in Germany," in Robert Wolfe, ed., *Americans as Proconsuls: United States Military Government in Germany and Japan, 1944–1952*, Carbondale, Ill.: Southern Illinois University Press, 1984, pp. 94–95.

[44] Ziemke (1984, p. 63).

[45] Schonberger (1989, p. 61).

[46] Earl F. Ziemke, *The U.S. Army in the Occupation of Germany, 1944–1946*, Washington, D.C.: U.S. Government Printing Office, 1990, p. 325.

[47] Ziemke (1990, pp. 324–325).

tact between Americans and Japanese. Seeing the behavior [that] the ordinary American soldier gave the Japanese, he said, "the opportunity for comparison between the qualities of the old and the new."[48]

This difference in fraternization policies illustrates the difference in Washington's influence on each occupation. In response to press criticism, General Marshall prohibited General Clay from relaxing the nonfraternization policy to a more reasonable level, whereas a U.S. lack of interest in the details of the occupation in Japan left MacArthur to run his own show. "Secretary of War Robert Patterson told a friend in July 1946 that MacArthur's administration of Japan was 'the one bright spot in postwar accomplishments [and the] spirit of the War Department was to let [SCAP] alone.'"[49] Personnel in Washington involved themselves in every facet of the occupation in Germany, and occupation officials in Germany were known to provide information to those in Washington outside the normal chains of command. Alternatively, everything that was transmitted between the SCAP and Washington, and vice versa, crossed MacArthur's desk.

> The cable traffic between Washington and Tokyo was only a fraction of that passing between Washington and Germany. In 1947, Colonel Charles Kades, then deputy chief of SCAP's Government Section, visited Washington and was offered the post of Deputy Assistant Secretary of State for Occupied Germany. To familiarize him with his responsibilities he was shown the enormous detail that he would have to supervise and declined the appointment. Nobody would have tried to manage MacArthur that way.[50]

---

[48] Cohen (1987, p. 123).

[49] Schonberger (1989, p. 61).

[50] Cohen (1987, p. 73).

Transition

During the North African occupation early in the war, civil affairs matters not related to security were initially delegated to the civilian North African Economic Board, but it quickly became clear that no civilian agency had the resources or personnel to conduct civil affairs operations, and the mission was given entirely to the military for the following liberations and occupations. But the U.S. government was uneasy with military officers involved in governing, even in occupied territories. Many claimed that it was imperialistic; others feared that it would endanger civilian control of the military. Throughout June and July 1945, the Department of War and DOS feuded over the limits of the Army's power in the occupation. DOS wanted to make policy and have the War Department administer and fund the occupation. The War Department wanted to perform only limited policing functions. Truman sided with the DOS view, agreeing that DOS was not prepared to assume the responsibility for the occupation, and the military remained in charge.[51] This effort to transfer control from military to civilian leadership would continue for four years before a U.S. civilian took overall responsibility for the German occupation. During that time, the proportion of civilian members to military members of the occupation grew, and the organization morphed slowly from military to civilian.

In the fall of 1945, the G-5 (civil affairs) section of USFET became the staff of the Office of Military Government of the United States (OMGUS). The military governor, initially, Eisenhower, was the head of OMGUS. Eisenhower was replaced in November 1945 by General Joseph T. McNarney, who, like Eisenhower, left the job of managing the occupation to General Clay, his deputy. In March 1947, Clay assumed the role of military governor and head of OMGUS. In May 1949, Clay was replaced as military governor by a civilian, John J. McCloy, who had been the Assistant Secretary of War in charge of military government planning, preparations, and operations throughout the war. Under McCloy, OMGUS became the Office of the U.S.

---

[51] Gimbel (1984, p. 93); Zink (1957, p. 43).

High Commissioner for Germany in late 1949, and control was effectively passed from the military to a civilian. Later, the third high commissioner, James B. Conant, became the first U.S. ambassador to the Federal Republic of Germany.[52]

In late 1947, the occupation in Japan shifted focus from reform to recovery in what would become known as the *reverse course*. Through the process of developing this new policy, several "missions" visited Japan to see the situation for themselves. In March 1948, MacArthur told Under Secretary of the Army William H. Draper, Jr., that "he opposed any plans that the Army Department might have for changing to a civilian regime of control for the remainder of the occupation." Later, in June 1949, Army Chief of Staff Omar Bradley wrote to MacArthur that "the 'trend of thought' in Washington was to get the State Department to proceed in Japan as it had done in Germany and appoint a civilian High Commissioner." MacArthur used this information to head off the effort, and, by September, Secretary of State Dean Acheson reassured him that there were no plans to make changes to the SCAP structure. The focus of DOS would be on the final peace treaty and the end of the occupation. In April 1950, John Foster Dulles was appointed special adviser to DOS for the peace treaty. MacArthur and Dulles worked together on this effort until MacArthur was relieved of his duty by President Truman over their public conflict about the prosecution of the Korean War. In April 1952, the peace treaty was signed and the occupation of Japan ended.[53]

Conclusion

Roosevelt organized his administration such that he would be able to control key decisions himself. He amplified the already competitive interagency environment by positioning his cabinet members against one another, all but destroying any tendency toward coordination and cooperation among departments. He tended to keep his own counsel

---

[52] Zink (1957, pp. 29, 31, 43, 76–78); Gimbel (1984, pp. 93, 95).

[53] Schonberger (1989, pp. 78, 84–86).

and leave decisions to the last possible minute to retain maximum control of their outcomes. In light of this lack of top-down guidance, what planning did occur for the postwar period was abundant but somewhat uncoordinated and contradictory.

Many high-level policy issues were not resolved in the planning process but were managed during the occupations themselves. The occupations in Germany and Japan unfolded in different ways. The differences were driven by the level of interest in United States—"Europe first" had been the hallmark of U.S. strategy from the beginning of the war—the personalities of the military governors and their priorities for the occupations; the comparative levels of destruction of the occupied territories; and, perhaps most importantly, the requirement to coordinate efforts with allies in Germany and not in Japan. In Germany, all the old national institutions were dismantled and new ones developed only slowly, over a period of years. In Japan, by contrast, all national institutions except the army and navy were kept, continued to function, and were reformed in place.

The contrasting nature of the occupations is also reflected in how the occupations transitioned to international integration in Germany and Japan. In Germany, there was a gradual transition from U.S. military control to U.S. civilian control to German sovereignty. In Japan, it was an easier transition from U.S. military control to Japanese sovereignty. Thus, until 1949, Germany had no national government. In Japan, by contrast, nearly all elements of the national government, from the emperor on down, were retained and reformed from within. This process of co-option worked much more rapidly and smoothly than the process of deconstruction and reconstruction of national institutions in Germany. On the other hand, the transformation of Germany into a fully democratic state, reconciled with its neighbors and its own historical responsibilities, was more thoroughgoing than that in Japan.

The cases of Germany and Japan show that several factors affect U.S. decisionmaking in nation-building. Organizational process and structure have major effects on outcomes. Likewise, personalities and politics, both domestic and international, had a significant impact on how these missions were crafted and executed. The reality on the ground in the nation to be rebuilt cannot be overemphasized as a driver of the success or failure of a mission—or its relative cost. Yet the fact is that the situations encountered by U.S. nation-builders in Germany and Japan were very different, as were some of the policies that followed, but the results were in both cases were remarkably successful—more successful, in fact, than in any subsequent case.

The success of the German and Japanese occupations had much to do with the fact that both countries had been devastatingly defeated, both governments had surrendered, both economies were highly advanced, and both societies were ethnically homogeneous (in the German case, due in part to Nazi genocide and the large-scale population transfers that accompanied the war's end). Few of these conditions would be met in subsequent U.S. endeavors to reform and rebuild war-torn societies.

CHAPTER FOUR

Post–Cold War Nation-Building: Somalia, Haiti, Bosnia, and Kosovo

Over the subsequent 40 years, successive U.S. administrations made few attempts to replicate the early nation-building successes in Germany and Japan. During the Cold War, U.S. policy emphasized containment, deterrence, and maintenance of the status quo. Efforts were made to promote democratic and free-market values but, generally, without the element of compulsion. U.S. military power was employed to preserve the status quo, not to alter it, to manage crises, not to resolve the underlying problems, lest doing so provoke a nuclear confrontation with the Soviet Union. Germany, Korea, Vietnam, China, Cyprus, and Palestine were divided. U.S. and international forces were used to maintain these and other divisions, not to compel resolution of the underlying disputes or unify the nations involved. U.S. interventions in such places as the Dominican Republic, Lebanon, Grenada, and Panama were short lived, undertaken to overthrow unfriendly regimes and reinstall friendly ones rather than bring about fundamental societal transformations.

The end of the Cold War and the demise of the Soviet Union brought new opportunities for the United States. U.S. power was no longer counterbalanced by that of a peer competitor. Multinational military action to preserve international peace and security became feasible, and the UN Security Council (UNSC) began to function as its founders had intended in mandating such missions. But the demand for such operations grew much more quickly than did the supply of national contingents with which to staff them, and calls on U.S.

resources soon exceeded the willingness of the public or Congress to make such commitments.

In the early 1990s, the United States struggled to find a foreign-policy focus. With the demise of an existential threat to the Western world, was the United States faced with *The End of History*,[1] or would the next period reflect *A Clash of Civilizations*[2] (to borrow the titles of two widely cited books of the period)? With the split of the Soviet Union and the reunification of Germany, challenges that had monopolized U.S. foreign-policy attention for half a century no longer took center stage. Other problems, such as humanitarian crises and ethnic war, which would have previously been viewed through the bipolar lens of the Cold War, became significant foreign-policy issues. Whether they were of vital interest to the United States would be debated throughout the 1990s, but U.S. interventions in Somalia, Haiti, Bosnia, and Kosovo would dominate the decade's foreign-policy landscape.

The Presidents and Their Administrations

As discussed earlier, administrations tend to reflect the personalities of their presidents. In contrast to Roosevelt's administration, which promoted competition, President George H. W. Bush forged an administration that placed a priority on a collegial exchange of ideas, relying on solid analysis and formal decisionmaking. It is routinely cited as the "model of a well-functioning NSC and interagency process."[3]

Bush himself had vast executive- and legislative-branch experience prior to assuming the presidency. In addition to eight years as vice president, he had previously been director of the CIA, mission chief in Beijing, and ambassador to the UN. He had also served in Congress, was a former U.S. Navy officer, and had chaired the Republican

---

[1] Francis Fukuyama, *The End of History and the Last Man*, New York: Free Press, 1992.

[2] Samuel Huntington, *Clash of Civilizations and the Remaking of World Order*, New York: Simon and Schuster, 1996.

[3] David J. Rothkopf, *Running the World: The Inside Story of the National Security Council and the Architects of American Power*, New York: Public Affairs, 2005, p. 261.

National Committee. Few presidents, if any, have had as extensive an exposure to national security affairs prior to assuming the presidency.

In terms of personality, Bush's cognitive style was almost in the middle of the spectrum. In discussing his views on the role of the cabinet, he noted, "I want them to be frank; I want them to fight hard for their position. And when I make the call, I'd like to have the feeling that they'd be able to support the president."[4] This indicates a certain belief in the importance of competition and argument among advisers.

At the same time, however, Bush also chose advisers with whom he had a personal relationship, and many had relationships to one another as well. President Bush, Secretary of State James Baker, Secretary of Defense Dick Cheney (Bush's second choice, after the Senate failed to confirm John Tower), and National Security Advisor Brent Scowcroft all had previously served together in the administration of President Gerald Ford. These personal relationships limited the worst forms of competition between advisers and agencies.[5]

Bush also assembled a group of competent but low-key personnel on the White House staff. The exception was Chief of Staff John Sununu, who could be domineering. Sununu's control was such that Bush reportedly had to open a post office box to ensure that various advisers could contact him when Sununu blocked their access. Overall, however, Bush's White House provided him with competent support and analysis without seeking to dominate the Cabinet agencies.[6]

Overall, George H. W. Bush's presidency can be characterized as fitting the collegial model. However, it was more structured and somewhat more competitive than the administration of President John F. Kennedy. This produced a smoothly functioning, but not totally insular, decisionmaking process for a president who knew much about the world and was on a first-name basis with many of its key leaders. He can be characterized as having a flexible but structured cognitive style, a strong sense of his own efficacy as manager of international affairs, and a tolerance for some competition among advisers.

---

[4] Hess and Pfiffner (2002, p. 150).

[5] Hess and Pfiffner (2002, pp. 148–150).

[6] Hess and Pfiffner (2002, pp. 152–155).

Key players in the Clinton transition, who had previously served in the Carter administration, recognized that a highly adversarial interagency system had not worked well and that the system set up under George H. W. Bush was more successful. As a result, and in contrast to past experience in presidential transitions, most of the Bush NSC structure and some key staffers at both the NSC and DOS were carried over into the Clinton administration. Even within the Bush structure, however, the Clinton administration's national security process tended to reflect his more "free-wheeling," informal approach to decisionmaking.

President Clinton was, in some ways, the opposite of President Bush in terms of international relations experience and personal style. In contrast to Bush's wide foreign experience and varied executive-branch service, Clinton was a former governor who had focused his campaign on domestic policy. Although his undergraduate degree was in international relations and he studied abroad, Clinton's initial interests and priorities were dominantly domestic. He was articulate and empathetic where Bush was prone to verbal gaffes and appeared to some to be distant.[7]

In terms of leadership style, Clinton initially did not delegate as well as Bush. He gave very little formal authority to his first chief of staff, in effect attempting to do the job himself. Clinton was very bright and sought to be intimately involved in the crafting of policy but was still initially more interested in domestic rather than foreign policy. He can be characterized as having a flexible cognitive style characterized by an ability to manage large amounts of information, a sense of his own efficacy in terms of policy detail, and a comfort with conflict among his advisers higher than that of Bush but much lower than that of Roosevelt.

Both Bush and Clinton inherited the executive structure initially implemented during the Truman presidency. The National Security Act of 1947 created the NSC to "advise the President with respect to the integration of domestic, foreign, and military policies relating to the national security so as to enable the military services and the

---

[7]   Hess and Pfiffner (2002, p. 147).

other departments and agencies of the Government to cooperate more effectively in matters involving the national security."[8] The NSC's membership traditionally includes the president, vice president, secretary of state, and secretary of defense, with the director of central intelligence and chair of the JCS acting as advisers. The original role of the assistant to the president for national security affairs was to be the head of the NSC staff. That role has expanded to include chairing meetings of NSC principals (in effect, NSC meetings without the president), acting as an "honest broker" in the interagency process, and providing national security advice to the president.

The scope of members and issues that fall under the purview of the NSC has grown since 1947. During the Bush administration, the President's Chief of Staff attended NSC meetings, and the Secretary of the Treasury was expected to attend unless specifically asked not to. The Attorney General, as well as any other department or agency head, special adviser, or senior official, would be invited when appropriate.[9] President Clinton further expanded the scope of the NSC to include the Secretary of the Treasury, the U.S. Representative to the United Nations, the Assistant to the President for National Security Affairs, the Assistant to the President for Economic Policy, and the President's Chief of Staff as full members of the NSC.[10]

President Bush established the NSC Principals Committee (NSC/PC) as the senior interagency forum for national security policy issues. It was charged with reviewing, coordinating, and monitoring the development and implementation of national security policy. Bush's NSC/PC was comprised of the Secretary of State, Secretary of Defense, Director of Central Intelligence, Chair of the JCS, and the Chief of Staff to the President and was chaired by the Assistant to the President for National Security Affairs. Others would be invited to participate

---

[8]   Rothkopf (2005, p. 5). See also Public Law 80-235, National Security Act of 1947, July 26, 1947.

[9]   George H. W. Bush, National Security Directive 1: Organization of the National Security Council System, Washington, D.C.: White House, January 30, 1989, p. 2.

[10] William J. Clinton, Presidential Decision Directive 2: Organization of the National Security Council, Washington, D,C.: White House, January 20, 1993a.

when appropriate. Clinton's NSC/PC added the U.S. Representative to the UN and the National Security Advisor to the Vice President. [11]

Below the NSC/PC was the NSC Deputies Committee (NSC/DC), established as a senior, subcabinet, interagency forum and charged with reviewing and monitoring the interagency process and making recommendations on the development and implementation of national security policy. Membership included the Under Secretary of Defense for Policy, the Under Secretary of State for Political Affairs, the Deputy Director of Central Intelligence, and the Vice Chair of the JCS and was chaired by the Deputy Assistant to the President for National Security Affairs. Others would be invited when appropriate. Clinton's NSC/DC included the Assistant to the Vice President for National Security Affairs. Bush's NSC/DC had standing NSC policy coordination committees in six regional and four functional areas, most of which were chaired by DOS at the assistant secretary level. Clinton's NSC/DC was authorized to establish permanent or ad hoc interagency working groups (IWGs).[12]

Within these formal structures, different groups emerged as engines of interagency collaboration in their respective administrations. Under President Bush, the NSC/DC was the workhorse of the interagency process. Chaired by Deputy National Security Advisor Robert Gates, the committee was made of department representatives who had the trust of their principals to commission and vet analysis, as well as to develop policy options that were not mere regurgitations of departmental positions. The deputies, having known each other through multiple presidential administrations, trusted each other to work together and find policy options that would work.[13] In the Clinton administration, the NSC/DC was supplemented by specially created executive committees (EXCOMs), which managed a good deal of the heavy interagency work, particularly in the cases of Somalia,

---

[11] Bush (1989); Clinton (1993a).

[12] Bush (1989); Clinton (1993a).

[13] Ivo H. Daalder and I. M. Destler, "The Bush Administration National Security Council," *The National Security Council Project: Oral History Roundtables*, Washington, D.C.: Brookings Institution, April 29, 1999, pp. 11–15.

Haiti, Bosnia, and Kosovo.[14] However, the President had to make a decision to act during an unfolding crisis before an EXCOM could be established, so the early work in developing policy options concerning whether to act was done through the preexisting structure. These early policy options tended to reflect departmental or agency positions, driving the President to choose between, for example, the DOS position and that of the Department of Defense (DoD), rather than from a selection of integrated policy options.

In addition to the disintegration of the Soviet Union, German reunification, the Gulf War, and extensive arms-control negotiations, the Bush administration also faced unfolding crises in Somalia, Haiti, and Yugoslavia. Without the overarching conflict of east versus west that had existed throughout the Cold War, deciding whether to intervene in a crisis became a more complicated, if, perhaps, less weighty, calculation. The stakes for the United States were lower than they had been in the Cold War, and the country was considering military interventions where it had no vital interests. However, because the United States had emerged from the Cold War as the lone remaining superpower, other countries looked to it to provide leadership and to intervene, and the United States was willing, in some cases, to take that role, so long as its interests were high enough and the risks were low enough.

Somalia

In January 1991, Somali dictator Siad Barre fled that country and, by November 1991, Somalia was wracked by open clan warfare. The U.S. Agency for International Development (USAID) and the International Committee of the Red Cross began reporting on the unfolding humanitarian crisis and, by the summer of 1992, there was a general consensus that somewhere between one-third and two-thirds of the Somali

---

[14] Ivo H. Daalder and I. M. Destler, "The Clinton Administration National Security Council," *The National Security Council Project: Oral History Roundtables*, Washington, D.C.: Brookings Institution, September 27, 2000, p. 13.

population was in "imminent danger of dying from malnutrition."[15] Somalis were starving, less from a lack of food than from a failure of the distribution system. Food had replaced currency as the source of wealth in Somalia, warring clans hijacked shipments, and relief aid was soon rotting in the port of Mogadishu because a lack of security prevented its safe distribution to those in need. In April 1992, the UNSC met to discuss options in Somalia. Due to U.S. resistance to paying for a large peacekeeping mission (the U.S. share at that time was approximately 30 percent of the total mission cost), the UNSC approved the deployment of a small force of 50 peacekeepers to Mogadishu—UN Operation in Somalia (UNOSOM). Unfortunately, the peacekeepers would not be on the ground until September, and once in place, they proved to be wholly ineffective.

Interagency Planning and the Decision to Intervene

In July 1992, President Bush read a cable from U.S. Ambassador to Kenya Smith Hempstone, Jr., that eloquently described the situation unfolding on the border between Somalia and Kenya, to which many refugees had fled. President Bush wrote in the margin, "This is a terribly moving situation. Let's do everything we can to help."[16] On August 12, Bush met with his Secretary of State, Secretary of Defense, and National Security Advisor and decided to airlift food into Kenya and Somalia and provide air transport to a larger contingent of 500 UN peacekeepers. Once again, the response would take time, and it was October before the airlift began.[17]

On November 3, President Bush lost his reelection campaign to Bill Clinton; however, he did not sit idly by in the last months of his presidency. On November 20–24, the NSC/DC met daily to discuss options for Somalia, and Ambassador Hempstone wrote another cable that captured in one sentence the challenges of military intervention in Somalia: "If you liked Beirut, you'll love Mogadishu." The NSC/DC

---

[15] Maryann K. Cusimano, *Operation Restore Hope: The Bush Administration's Decision to Intervene in Somalia*, Washington, D.C.: Institute for the Study of Diplomacy, 1995, p. 4.

[16] Cusimano (1995, p. 5).

[17] Cusimano (1995, p. 6).

crafted three policy options for the President, which were presented at a November 25 NSC meeting that included the President, National Security Advisor Brent Scowcroft, Director of Central Intelligence Robert Gates, Secretary of Defense Dick Cheney, and Chairman of the JCS General Colin Powell. The three policy options developed by the committee were as follows:

- Status quo plus: Continue to aid and support an increased UN presence.
- U.S. support to an international coalition: Propose an international coalition under UN command and control with U.S. airlift, sealift, logistic, and communication support.
- U.S. military mission: Send one or more U.S. divisions of ground troops under U.S. command and control into Somalia to provide security for food distribution.

Scowcroft and Cheney advocated the third option, to send in a large contingent of U.S. troops. Powell was not a firm supporter of the third option but recommended against the second option.[18] President Bush chose the third option but wanted UN authorization for the use of force and an increase in the number of UN peacekeepers on the ground. Once security was regained, the UN commander would take responsibility for the operation, including the restoration of a working government in Somalia, with a smaller number of U.S. forces remaining in the country under UN command.

Implementation
That afternoon, President Bush directed acting Secretary of State Lawrence Eagleburger to go to the UN and present the U.S. plan for Somalia. The U.S. military mission would be limited to security only, while the UN would be responsible for the more complex task of assisting Somalia in reestablishing a government. The UNSC unanimously passed Resolution 794 on December 3, 1992, which authorized "all necessary means to establish as soon as possible a secure environment

---

[18] Cusimano (1995, pp. 7–10).

for humanitarian relief operations."[19] Neither the United States nor the
UN defined a long-term strategy for Somalia, and this lack of guidance would result in contradictory actions on the ground in Somalia. President Bush announced the resolution and U.S. deployment on
December 4 and claimed that U.S. troops would be out of Somalia by
inauguration day. President-elect Clinton supported Bush's decision on
Somalia, but no one believed that U.S. troops would be out of Somalia
by the end of January. Chairman Powell had the most realistic assessment: that it would take three to six months to establish safe distribution routes before the UN could take over with a smaller number of
U.S. forces.

Unified Task Force (UNITAF) deployed to Mogadishu in December 1992 with overwhelming force. Comprised of 31,000 U.S. troops,
the mission was initially successful, establishing security and ensuring the delivery of much-needed humanitarian aid. Mohammed Farah
Aidid, the warlord in charge of the Mogadishu area, was publicly supportive of the U.S. deployment, thinking that he could play the United
States against UNOSOM, the UN mission that remained in place
with a larger complement of nearly 3,500 international peacekeepers,
to improve his position. As an agreed-to condition of the U.S. deployment, UNITAF and UNOSOM maintained separate lines of command and control. As intended, the initial large deployment of U.S.
forces quickly withdrew, and the United States reducing troop levels
to approximately 4,000 by March 1993. At the same time, other UN
members increased their troop levels in Somalia to nearly 20,000
under a Turkish general, and, in May, UNITAF officially ended and
UNOSOM II began, with 4,000 U.S. troops remaining under independent U.S. command.

Transition

As the Somalia mission transitioned from the limited-scope, U.S.-
dominated force to the wider UN multinational contingent, the newly
installed Clinton administration held no formal policy review. The

---

[19] Cusimano (1995, p. 11). See also UNSC Resolution 794, on the situation in Somalia,
December 3, 1992.

issue of differing U.S. and UN goals was never addressed, and U.S. troops on the ground in Somalia began seizing some of the larger clan weapon caches in support of the wider UN mission. Once UNITAF left Somalia in May, Aidid believed that it was time for him to act, and, on June 5, 1993, his forces attacked and killed 24 Pakistani UN troops patrolling in Mogadishu. In response, both UN and U.S. policy shifted to capturing or killing Aidid, which effectively closed the door to a diplomatic settlement with the clan leader and, as a result, a political settlement for Somalia—not that such a settlement would have been easy to achieve, in any case.

Still, top-level decisionmaking remained informal. Soon after Aidid's attack on the Pakistani troops, Chairman Powell brought a proposal to the President to support UNSC Resolution 837,[20] directing the arrest of Aidid, despite admitting that there was only a 50-percent chance that the warlord could be captured and only a 25-percent chance that he could be captured alive.[21] Clinton agreed, but there were no detailed discussions of how this policy shift would change U.S. military operations on the ground or how such a shift would support a larger strategy in Somalia. There still was no articulated long-term U.S. strategy for Somalia.

Throughout the summer, the situation in Somalia deteriorated. Forces had been unable to capture Aidid, Somali civilians were being caught in the cross-fire, and troops from individual member countries were making deals with Aidid's forces to not arrest them in exchange for their safety. The coalition was coming apart, and the United States tried to shift emphasis from the Aidid hunt back to a political solution to establish a government in Somalia. On August 8, four U.S. soldiers were killed in Mogadishu when their vehicle was blown up. In response, on September 9, the Senate passed a nonbinding resolution directing President Clinton to report U.S. goals and objectives in Somalia to Congress no later than October 15. Three weeks later, the House of Representatives adopted the same nonbinding resolution. In response, the ad hoc policy review continued, with Secretary of Defense

---

[20] UNSC Resolution 837, on the situation in Somalia, June 6, 1993.

[21] William J. Clinton, *My Life*, New York: Alfred A. Knopf, 2004, p. 550.

Les Aspin declaring three conditions for a U.S. withdrawal: "First, the security issue in south Mogadishu must be settled. Second, we must make real progress towards taking the heavy weapons out of the hands of the warlords. And third, there must be credible police forces in at least the major population centers." Secretary of State Warren Christopher wrote to UN Secretary-General Boutros Boutros-Ghali, expressing the desire to position the remaining U.S. troops in Somalia on ships at sea instead of on the ground in Somalia.[22] In response, Boutros-Ghali wrote that the proposal would return Somalia to civil war and undermine the UN.

The U.S. desire to move away from capturing Aidid was never transmitted to forces in the field, who, when they joined in the hunt for Aidid, had themselves become targets. On October 3, Aidid's forces in Mogadishu killed 18 U.S. soldiers—an event vividly described in Mark Bowden's book *Black Hawk Down* and later in a film of the same name.[23] In response, the Clinton NSC convened its first meeting on Somalia on October 5. Three options were presented to the President:

- Stay the course: Deploy additional troops and another diplomatic mission to pressure resolution on the development of a central government in Somalia.
- Immediate withdrawal: Immediately withdraw all U.S. troops from UNOSOM.
- A bit of both: Initially increase the U.S. troop presence, to be followed by a phased withdrawal of U.S. troops over a period of six months and a firm exit date, in combination with a diplomatic mission to press for resolution on the issue of a central government.

On October 7, President Clinton announced that the United States would increase its troop strength in Somalia, up to approxi-

---

[22] Ivo H. Daalder, *The Clinton Administration and Multilateral Peace Operations*, Washington, D.C.: Institute for the Study of Diplomacy, 1994, pp. 8–9.

[23] Mark Bowden, *Black Hawk Down: A Story of Modern War*, Berkeley, Calif.: Atlantic Monthly Press, 1999.

mately 5,300 troops on the ground, with the addition of heavy armor and an aircraft carrier off the coast. He also announced that all U.S. forces would be withdrawn by March 31, 1994, and that Ambassador Robert Oakley was being sent to Somalia to diplomatically push for a political settlement. Additional U.S. troops deployed and strengthened defensive positions at the air- and seaports in Mogadishu. Ambassador Oakley, despite intense efforts, was unable to broker an agreement between the clan leaders and, through his willingness to negotiate with Aidid, alienated the UN. U.S. troops began a phased withdrawal, and all troops were removed before the self-imposed March 31 deadline. Other nations followed suit, and UNOSOM ended on March 31, 1995.[24] While the famine in Somalia was averted, the country still has no central government and remains a chaotic, ungoverned nation wracked by clan warfare—the very epitome of a failed state.

President Bush and his national security team developed a short-term response to a humanitarian crisis, but once U.S. troops had established security and turned the mission over to the UN to develop a political settlement, the United States failed to conduct a formal policy review. The early months of the Clinton administration were busy, with the President focused more on domestic issues than international ones and new staffs taking their places and learning their jobs. Nancy Soderberg, Clinton's first NSC staff director, said, "On Somalia, the problem was a failure to see that the situation was not going well. The reason there were no principals meetings on Somalia before that was that everybody thought it was going well."[25] There was no system for interagency oversight of UNOSOM II that might have recognized unfolding problems and policy contradictions. Ultimately, the short-term success in overcoming the famine was lost in the long-term failure to create a government in Somalia, and lessons from Somalia would color future U.S. interventions, some for the good, others not.

---

[24] Ken Menkhaus and Louis Ortmayer, *Key Decisions in the Somalia Intervention*, Washington, D.C.: Institute for the Study of Diplomacy, 1995, pp. 18–23.

[25] Rothkopf (2005, p. 335).

Presidential Decision Directive 25

Although the administration was not formally overseeing the Somalia mission at the interagency level, from the beginning of the Clinton administration, a formal review of the larger policy of U.S. participation in UN peacekeeping missions was undertaken. In early February 1993, President Clinton signed Presidential Review Directive (PRD) 13, which directed an interagency study of peace operations.[26]

> Its purpose was to devise a plan for the long-term strengthening of UN peace-keeping and U.S. capacity to participate. PRD-13's mandate was to examine U.S. participation in multilateral operations involving peacekeeping, humanitarian relief, observer groups, and enforcement of UN mandates (peace-enforcement). Specific topics to be reviewed included the overall role of peace-keeping, the role of regional organizations, the administrative and operational capabilities of the United Nations, financing, command and control mechanisms (including the role of Article 43 agreements and a possible UN stand-by force), the structure of the U.S. governmental organization supporting these activities, and the executive-legislative relationship.[27]

The review was initially conducted by an IWG chaired by NSC staffer Richard Clarke. Participants included representatives from DOS, DoD, JCS, the National Intelligence Council, the U.S. mission to the UN, and the Office of Management and Budget.

The PRD-13 IWG completed its decision paper, and a draft was circulated in May. The NSC/DC reviewed, directed changes to, and approved the decision paper, then directed the IWG to draft a document that would become Presidential Decision Directive (PDD) 25.[28] By July, the only item of contention in the draft PDD was whether

---

[26] William J. Clinton, Presidential Review Directive 13, Peacekeeping Operations, February 1993b. Not available to the general public.

[27] Daalder (1994, p. 4).

[28] William J. Clinton, Presidential Decision Directive 25, U.S. Policy on Reforming Multilateral Peace Operations, May 3, 1994.

DOS or DoD was responsible for paying for UN peacekeeping missions. A final draft of the PDD was approved by the NSC/DC on July 19, 1993, and, by early August, the contents of the draft were leaked to the *Washington Post*. In the face of public criticism of the draft policy, the NSC/PC met on September 17 to discuss the draft. The principals were unable to reach a consensus, with U.S. Ambassador to the UN Madeleine Albright supportive of an expanded UN peacekeeping role and Chairman Powell against, Secretary of State Warren Christopher not wishing to advocate any significant changes, Secretary of Defense Aspin supportive in theory but sensitive to the military view, and National Security Advisor Tony Lake worried that the issue of peacekeeping was going to hijack the entire Clinton foreign-policy agenda. The NSC/PC sent the draft back to the IWG for review.[29]

The IWG completed its review by the middle of November, but it was not until May 3, 1994, that PDD 25, U.S. Policy on Reforming Multilateral Peace Operations, was signed by the President after extensive consultations with members of Congress. PDD 25 laid out the following framework to both improve peacekeeping operations and assist U.S. decisionmaking in support of those operations:

- Support the right operations: Ensure that UN operations that the United States supports or in which it participates meet stringent criteria, including by determining whether the mission is in the United States' interest, whether there is a threat to international peace and security, whether there is a clear mandate, and whether there is a clear objective.
- Reduce costs: Reduce both the overall cost of UN peacekeeping missions and the U.S. share of those costs.
- Improve UN capabilities: Improve UN capabilities through enhanced planning, logistics, command and control, public affairs, intelligence, and policing.
- Clarify policy on command and control of U.S. forces: There should be no change in the previous policy that retains U.S.

---

[29] Daalder (1994, pp. 5, 9–10).

command of military forces but allows operational control to be shifted to international commanders.

- Improve U.S. management of peacekeeping operations: DOS and DoD should share responsibility, both policywise and financially, for peacekeeping operations.
- Improve cooperation with Congress: Improve the flow of information and consultation between Congress and the executive branch.[30]

For the first time, the United States had a formal framework for approaching the support of and participation in UN peacekeeping operations. The mission in Haiti would, as a result, prove a significant improvement over that in Somalia, though it too yielded little long-term benefit.

Haiti

In December 1990, Haiti had the first "free and fair" elections in its history, choosing as President Jean-Bertrand Aristide by an overwhelming majority. Only nine months later, on September 30, 1991, Aristide was overthrown by a military coup and forced to flee Haiti. The initial U.S. response was to call the coup a "threat to the national security, foreign policy, and economy of the United States." Clearly, in the mind of President Bush and Secretary of State James Baker, the maintenance of democracy in Haiti was an important, if not vital, national interest. If allowed to stand, Secretary of State Baker believed that it would result in a "chain reaction" through the region. The option of military force was quickly discarded—the military was reluctant to use force in Haiti in 1991—and the United States focused on other means of returning Aristide to power, including a joint trade embargo with the Organiza-

---

[30] Tony Lake and General Wesley Clark, "Reforming Multilateral Peace Operations (PDD 25) Press Briefing," Washington, D.C.: White House, May 5, 1994.

tion of American States, the forced repatriation of Haitian refugees, and pressuring Aristide to negotiate with the ruling junta.[31]

Interagency Planning and the Decision to Intervene

Clinton had campaigned in favor of yet tougher sanctions to force Aristide's restoration to power in Haiti, and, upon taking office, he appointed a special envoy for Haiti, Lawrence Pezzullo, and worked with the UN to increase sanctions against Haiti. This increasing economic pressure drove Raoul Cédras, the leader of the junta, to agree to UN- and Organization of American States–sponsored negotiations, which resulted in the Governors Island Accord, signed on July 3, 1993. The agreement called for the departure and amnesty of the coup leaders; sanctions to be lifted by October 30, 1993, the same day on which Aristide would return to power; and the expansion of the UN humanitarian mission to include training for the Haitian armed forces and the establishment of a new police force. In October, just a few days after the U.S. military debacle in Somalia, an advance force of U.S. and Canadian troops, deployed in support of the expanded UN mission, was dissuaded from landing by a small group of pro-junta demonstrators. In the wake of "Blackhawk down," Washington was unwilling to risk another such incident in Port-au-Prince. It was clear by then that the Governors Island Accord would not be implemented.[32]

Negotiations continued through the fall of 1993 and spring of 1994, but Aristide, who had been a reluctant participant at the Governors Island negotiations, refused to concede on many points. Within the Clinton administration, there continued to be strong advocates both for and against the use of force. Special envoy Lawrence Pezzullo, Secretary of Defense Les Aspin, Chair of the JCS Colin Powell, and CIA director James Woolsey were against the use of force, while administrative hawks included Vice President Al Gore, Secretary of State Warren Christopher, National Security Advisor Tony Lake, and U.S. Ambassador to the UN Madeleine Albright. The majority in Congress was

---

[31] Curtis H. Martin, *President Clinton's Haiti Dilemma: Trial by Failure*, Washington, D.C.: Institute for the Study of Diplomacy, 1997, pp. 1–2.

[32] Martin (1997, p. 3).

against the use of force in Haiti, with the Senate passing a nonbinding resolution on October 21, 1993, that required prior consultation with Congress before any military intervention in Haiti. Several other nonbinding resolutions requiring consultation with Congress over the use of military force in Haiti followed. One notable congressional exception was the Congressional Black Caucus, which had been an outspoken proponent of the use of force to restore democracy in Haiti.[33]

On April 22, 1994, the Clinton administration announced that it intended to seek a total embargo against Haiti and that "the use of force is not ruled out." In response to this shift in policy, special envoy Pezzullo resigned and was replaced by William Gray, a former member of Congress and former chair of the Congressional Black Caucus. By this point, Secretary of Defense Aspin had been fired, in part due to his handling of Somalia, to be replaced by his deputy, William Perry. Chairman Powell had retired and was succeeded by General John Shalikashvili. Both these new incumbents remained opposed to the use of force, but Secretary Perry nevertheless ordered DoD to begin interagency planning for a military intervention in Haiti.[34] On May 5, 1994, the UNSC tightened sanctions again, banning all but humanitarian imports to Haiti. The United States then convinced most of the countries in the western hemisphere to support military intervention in Haiti in the event that sanctions failed to return Aristide to power.

In May, the Haiti EXCOM was stood up under NSC leadership. It included representatives from DOS, DoD, the Justice Department, JCS, the Treasury Department, the CIA, and USAID.[35] A small group of planners at the U.S. Atlantic Command (USACOM), the regional headquarters responsible for Haiti, had been developing a military plan for Haiti designed to "synchronize official cooperation for a Haiti incursion." According to Lieutenant Colonel Ed Donnelly, an officer who worked on the plan,

---

[33] Martin (1997, pp. 4–6).

[34] Margaret Daly Hayes and Gary F. Wheatley, eds., *Interagency and Political-Military Dimensions of Peace Operations: Haiti—A Case Study*, Washington, D.C.: National Defense University, 1996, p. 5.

[35] Hayes and Wheatley (1996, p. 16).

USACOM essentially put together a document that told the Interagency Working Group within the National Security Council what [it] would be expected to contribute to an operation in Haiti. USACOM laid out the purpose of the operation, the endstate, and defined criteria for military success. That document went to the JCS and then the NSC where it was codified. The document then came back with corrections but essentially USACOM wrote the document.[36]

A larger group of USACOM planners developed parallel operational plans. First, in May, USACOM tasked the XVIII Airborne Corps to plan a forcible entry into Haiti. This plan would become Operations Plan (OPLAN) 2370. Later, in July, at the urging of the JCS, USACOM directed the XVIII Airborne Corps to develop a permissive-entry version of the plan, OPLAN 2380. Soon, however, USACOM would shift responsibility for OPLAN 2380 to the 10th Mountain Division. Military planning remained tightly compartmented and highly classified, frustrating those who knew that both plans would require coordination outside the narrow military chains of command and leaving the administration's civilian leadership largely in the dark. Throughout the summer, civilian agencies worked on their preparations for an intervention in Haiti, but they were

> unfamiliar with the concept and with the idea of establishing precise lines of command and control and timelines for execution of projects. The first-ever attempt at a political-military operational plan undertaken by State, [USAID], Justice, Treasury, etc. during the late summer improved comprehension substantially but was a far cry from the clarity and rigor of military planning.[37]

Civilian agencies were unused to detailed planning, and the military was refusing to share its own planning. As a result, this initial attempt at political-military planning had major gaps.

---

[36] Walter E. Kretchik, Robert F. Baumann, and John T. Fishel, *Invasion, Intervention, "Intervasion": A Concise History of the U.S. Army in Operation Uphold Democracy*, Ft. Leavenworth, Kan.: U.S. Army Command and General Staff College Press, 1998, p. 44.

[37] Hayes and Wheatley (1996, p. 16).

On July 31, 1994, UNSC Resolution 940 "authorized a U.S.-led force to use 'all means necessary to facilitate the departure of the military leadership' and to 'establish and maintain a secure and stable environment.'"[38] It called for a UN peacekeeping force to follow the U.S. force and take over responsibility for maintaining order, as well as to retrain the army and police and monitor elections. In August, Ambassador Albright told the ruling junta in Haiti, "You have a choice. You can depart voluntarily and soon, or you can depart involuntarily and soon."[39] The junta chose the second option.

Throughout the summer, military planners continued to update and refine OPLANs 2370 and 2380. On September 2, 1994, 10th Mountain Division and XVIII Airborne Corps planners were brought together at USACOM and directed to develop a third plan, OPLAN 2375, that would bridge the gap between the forcible-entry and the permissive-entry options. Planners worked feverishly to develop options while forces were moved into place and readied to execute either OPLAN 2370 or OPLAN 2380.

On September 12, 1994, the Haiti IWG was convened to conduct a final rehearsal of the previously agreed-to political-military plan, allowing each agency and department to brief its part of the plan for the mission in Haiti. USACOM planners revealed little of their own planning for the invasion and instead sought to focus on what would be expected of other agencies.

> At one point, [USACOM planner Major General Michael] Byron turned to the Department of Justice representative to explain just how that department was going to train and equip the new Haitian Police force. The Department of Justice representative stated [that] the department could not handle the mission.[40]

---

[38] UNSC Resolution 940, on authorization to form a multinational force under unified command and control to restore the legitimately elected president and authorities of the government of Haiti and extensions of the mandate of the UN Mission in Haiti, July 31, 1994.

[39] Martin (1997, p. 6).

[40] Kretchik, Baumann, and Fishel (1998, p. 71).

One senior player noted: "We tried to do the interagency coordination on September 12, but it was a disaster." There were too many people for real candor. "People just recited what they were doing." A senior military officer expressed alarm, reportedly observing, "This is the kind of planning that gets people killed."[41]

A smaller IWG meeting was convened the following day, and most of the issues were worked out, but the political-military review would prove to be an eye-opening example of how far civil-military coordination still had to go and how incompatible it was with the strict operational security limitations that the military normally imposed on the dissemination of military plans to civilians.

Implementation

There were now three separate OPLANs with different command arrangements and forces in place to execute any of them when ordered. On September 15, President Clinton addressed the nation, explaining that, if the junta did not leave Haiti immediately, the United States would lead a multinational force to forcibly remove it and restore the democratically elected Aristide to power. While not publicized, Clinton had set midnight on September 18 as the deadline. After his televised address, he asked former President Jimmy Carter, retired General Colin Powell, and Senator Sam Nunn to fly to Haiti to try one last time to peacefully resolve the situation.[42] They arrived in Haiti on September 16, with Carter engaging with junta leader Raoul Cédras, Nunn trying to convince the Haitian parliament, and Powell talking with Haitian military leaders. On September 17, Clinton reviewed the invasion plan with the Chair of the JCS and the commander of USACOM.[43] On September 18, the Secretary of Defense signed the executive order for OPLAN 2370 (for an opposed entry), and planes began taking off later that evening, headed for their drop zones in Haiti. Carter called Clinton and told him that an agreement had been reached, the invasion was

---

[41] Hayes and Wheatley (1996, p. 15).

[42] Martin (1997, pp. 9–10).

[43] Clinton (2004, pp. 616–617).

stood down, and the planes returned to their bases. Late on the night of September 18, military planners were once again told to develop a plan, called OPLAN 2380-Plus, that would have the OPLAN 2380 permissive-entry forces deploy on the following day but in an ambiguous, less-than-permissive, threat environment. In just a few hours, OPLAN 2380 was altered, and General Hugh Shelton, commanding officer of the XVIII Airborne Corps, landed in Haiti to meet with Cédras to discuss the modalities of the junta's departure.[44]

Because of the ambiguous conditions on the ground and poor intelligence, the military forces did not know how they would be received by the Haitian military or the local population. They had planned to take down the military in the opening days of the invasion. Now, under the negotiated settlement, they would be using the army and police (who were part of the army) to help maintain order throughout the country. Initially, the local population was confused and dismayed, believing that the U.S. military would come in and get rid of the locally unpopular Haitian military but then saw the two forces collaborating. In an incident on the first day of the mission, a group of U.S. Army soldiers stood by while Haitian police attacked a group of civilians who had come out to cheer the U.S. forces, beating one to death and dispersing the others. In a separate incident only four days later, a U.S. Marine patrol came upon a group of Haitian police who, the patrol leader thought, were reaching for their weapons. The Marines preempted and 10 Haitians were killed. The rules of engagement were vague and interpreted differently by the Army and Marines. Both incidents strained relations, first between the United States and the local population, second between the Haitian and U.S. militaries. The rules of engagement were reviewed, and only minor incidents of violence followed, with overall security maintained throughout the country. However, the two incidents were widely reported by the media.[45]

The 10th Mountain Division had recently served in Somalia, and many of the lessons learned there were employed in Haiti, whether they

[44] Kretchik, Baumann, and Fishel (1998, p. 76).

[45] Kretchik, Baumann, and Fishel (1998, p. 98).

applied or not. Understandably, force protection was a primary priority for the Army commanders. Security at the base in Port-au-Prince was incredibly tight—so much so that the civil-military operations center on base could not function effectively. Many international civilians and local Haitians could not get access. U.S. civil affairs officers started to work out of the Haiti Assistance Coordination Center, located outside the U.S. base. The 10th Mountain soldiers were initially to remain inside their garrison. It took a great amount of effort and direction from higher headquarters to get the troops out on regular patrols throughout the city, interacting with the local population.[46] In contrast, the Marines in the area around Cap-Hatien immediately began patrolling and developing relationships with the local population.

The military forces made a conscious decision from the beginning to not engage in missions that could be construed as nation-building. Once again, the lessons from Somalia applied, and the military was afraid of mission creep. It took the direct order of the commander of USACOM to get U.S. troops on the ground to assist the Haitians in restoring electricity and clean water.[47] The military incorrectly expected the civilian development experts to be on the ground immediately after the deployment of U.S. troops and money to start flowing in for development projects. Neither expectation was fulfilled. While there were a significant number of official U.S. and international civilians on the ground in Haiti when the military arrived—many international organizations had been operating there for some time and the U.S. embassy remained open throughout the crisis—it took additional time to expand the civilian presence, deploy international police, and initiate significant development projects.

Civilians who were deployed in support of the military intervention ran into their own set of problems. They could not get military flights into Haiti, and commercial aviation was disrupted. The military had not accounted for them in its planning, the military deployment system did not support the allocation of airlifts to interagency players, and the civilians did not know how to relay their requirements within the mili-

---

[46] Kretchik, Baumann, and Fishel (1998, pp. 106–108).

[47] Kretchik, Baumann, and Fishel (1998, p. 123).

tary system. Additionally, most civilian agencies do not have a ready pool of trained personnel ready to deploy at a moment's notice, as the military does. It simply took time to get people together and get them into Haiti.[48]

The issue that most divided DoD and DOS planners in the weeks leading up to the invasion, other than whether to conduct the operation at all, had been that of responsibility for public security. DoD insisted that the U.S. military would not conduct policing nor oversee those who did. This, it insisted, should be a DOS function. DOS responded by retaining Raymond Kelly, former New York City police commissioner, and recruiting 1,000 U.S. and international civilian police who were tasked with supervising local Haitian police forces, substitute for them when necessary, and mentoring new police officers as these were trained and deployed. DOS cautioned, however, that Kelly and his force would be deployed incrementally over the first couple of months of the U.S. deployment and would not be available in sufficient numbers during the early days of the intervention. DoD persisted in refusing to accept the public-security mission, even for this interval, until U.S. network cameras captured scenes of local police beating cheering Haitian demonstrators who had come to the port to greet arriving U.S. soldiers. The following day, hundreds of additional U.S. military police were dispatched to take control of the Haitian police.

Many military participants were frustrated that there was not one person in charge of the overall mission. In the case of Haiti, the U.S. ambassador there was in charge of all civilian operations, and the military commander was in charge of military operations. Although they worked closely together, the absence of any coordinating mechanism below made interagency coordination and follow-up more difficult.[49]

---

[48] Hayes and Wheatley (1996, p. 17).

[49] Hayes and Wheatley (1996, p. 19).

Transition

The UNSC passed Resolution 975, directing the transition from the multinational force to the UN Mission in Haiti (UNMIH) by March 31, 1995.[50] U.S. Army Major General Joseph Kinzer was appointed as military commander for UNMIH. He was dual hatted as the commander of the U.S. contingent of troops participating in the mission and the overall UN commander, in which capacity he reported directly to Lakhdar Brahimi, the head of UNMIH and the UN secretary-general's special representative. In early March, USACOM established a UN staff-training program to get the multinational UN military staff, many of whom were American, working together before they deployed to Haiti. In the transition from the multinational force to UNMIH, U.S. troop numbers were reduced to approximately 2,400. The UNMIH mandate was extended several times in six-month increments, and, by the end of 1995, U.S. troops ended their participation in UNMIH, with a Canadian general taking over the military command in Haiti.

On May 24, 1995, the National Defense University held the workshop Interagency and Political-Military Dimensions of Peace Operations to explore the lessons that could be gleaned from the recent experience in Haiti. The workshop participants agreed that the intervention in Haiti was a success based on the limited objectives that the United States had set for itself: depose the ruling junta, restore order, return the elected president to power, and turn the mission over to the UN within six months.[51] The workshop participants believed that the mission was successful because the planning had incorporated lessons learned from missions in Lebanon, Grenada, Panama, and Somalia; the Carter mission had ensured a permissive entry of U.S. forces; military forces were flexible and adapted planning up until the last minute; the quality of tactical-level interagency coordination was high; the United States took the lead in the initial mission, allowing the UN

---

[50] UNSC Resolution 975, on extension of the mandate of the UN Mission in Haiti and transfer of responsibility from the multinational force in Haiti to the UN Mission in Haiti, January 30, 1995.

[51] Hayes and Wheatley (1996, p. 12).

time to stand up a force to take over the mission; and international police monitors were available and used to fill the gap in police monitoring and training.[52]

Although the Haiti operation achieved all its objectives on schedule and without encountering significant opposition, the mission paid few lasting dividends. Haiti was too dysfunctional a polity to be repaired within the short time that the United States and the rest of the international community were prepared to devote to the task. The American body politic had concluded from the Somali trauma that future military interventions should avoid mission creep, be launched with an exit strategy, and set an early departure deadline. All three lessons were followed in Haiti, and the result was ultimate failure, with the United States and the UN having to intervene again a decade later, in 2004.

Despite the initial success of the mission, the workshop participants agreed, even in its immediate aftermath, that much could be improved upon. They listed several significant problems with the interagency planning for Haiti: The high-level policy debate delayed planning, operational-level coordination was incomplete, interagency logistical support was initially confused, civil-military coordination was incomplete, coordination between the military and nongovernmental organizations (NGOs)/private voluntary organizations (PVOs) was incomplete, civilian-military command arrangements were ad hoc, and the rules of engagement were ambiguous.[53] Overall, five interagency lessons learned were proposed at the workshop:

- An interagency planning doctrine for complex emergencies is needed.
- Planning must compensate for organizational and operational differences between civilian and military organizations.
- Agreement on interagency command-and-control arrangements is needed.

---

[52] Hayes and Wheatley (1996, p. 13).

[53] Hayes and Wheatley (1996, p. 14).

- Agreement is needed on operational concepts for operations other than war.
- Interagency war games can help work out interagency differences and give agencies exposure to each other.[54]

Many of these lessons would be reviewed later and integrated into planning doctrine but not until many of the same lessons were learned again in the U.S. intervention in Bosnia.

Bosnia

Yugoslavia had slowly started to fall apart after the 1980 death of communist leader Josip Broz Tito, but in 1989, after the Berlin Wall fell, Yugoslavia began its disintegration in earnest, with states beginning to openly challenge the central government. On June 25, 1991, just days after Secretary of State James Baker visited Belgrade, the states of Slovenia and Croatia declared their independence, and on June 27, the latest Balkan War began and soon to center itself in the former Yugoslav republic of Bosnia. David Gompert, then an NSC staff member, wrote, "The Bush national security team that performed so well in other crises was divided and stumped." National Security Advisor Brent Scowcroft and Deputy Secretary of State Lawrence Eagleburger had both served in Yugoslavia earlier in their careers and were concerned about what was unfolding, but they saw no way to stop it. Secretary of State Baker did not think that important U.S. interests were involved and declared, "We don't have a dog in this fight."[55] President Bush and Baker felt that Europe could solve the problem. Chair of the JCS Colin Powell's view was that, if the United States wanted to do anything in Bosnia, it would need at least 200,000 troops:[56]

---

[54] Hayes and Wheatley (1996, p. 22).

[55] Richard Holbrooke, *To End a War*, New York: Modern Library, 1999, pp. 26–27.

[56] Rothkopf (2005, p. 325).

Yugoslavia was not an issue that we thought was either ripe for resolution, susceptible to the use of force, or warranted what it would require in order for us to have a hope in hell of making a difference. This was a shared view at the top . . . not focused in any one agency.[57]

Throughout the election year of 1992, Bill Clinton criticized the Bush administration's policy on Bosnia, and, once elected, President Clinton's first PRD called for a review of U.S. Bosnia policy.[58] Whereas the Bush administration had been unified in its passive policy—at least at the top—the Clinton administration's senior leaders were soon deadlocked by opposing views, with DOS favoring a more active role and DoD opposed. With Powell's prediction that an operation to stop the violence in Bosnia would involve a large number of casualties, the Bush policy of allowing Europe to deal with Bosnia continued for more than a year into the Clinton administration. Former Secretary of State Cyrus Vance and former British Foreign Secretary David Owen, representing the UN and the European Community, respectively, developed a peace plan that would divide Bosnia into 10 semiautonomous and largely ethnically homogenous cantons. The international effort in Bosnia was focused on getting the warring parties to agree to the Vance-Owen plan. The Clinton administration did not regard the plan as an enforceable solution to the war in Bosnia but was unwilling to take over the peace process from the Europeans or contribute to the UN peacekeeping force, which was trying to limit the violence and protect the civilian population.[59]

Interagency Planning and the Decision to Intervene

The debate on U.S. Bosnia policy largely took place in the NSC/PC, with National Security Advisor Tony Lake acting as "honest broker." With Muslim and Croat willingness to sign on to the Vance-Owen

---

[57] Daalder and Destler (1999, pp. 25, 27).

[58] Rothkopf (2005, p. 364).

[59] Ivo H. Daalder, *Getting to Dayton: The Making of America's Bosnia Policy*, Washington, D.C.: Brookings Institution Press, 2000, pp. 9–11.

plan, continued Serb intransigence, the situation on the ground in Bosnia rapidly deteriorating, and increasing pressure from both Congress and the U.S. public to do something, by April 1993, the committee developed a "lift-and-strike" plan, whereby the arms embargo against Bosnia would be lifted and U.S. or NATO air strikes against Serb positions would force the warring parties to agree to serious negotiations. Europe had been consistently against lifting the arms embargo, and, when Secretary of State Warren Christopher took the lift-and-strike plan to the European allies in May to ask for their support, the answer was no. Nor were they keen on having the United States conducting air operations against the Serbs while European troops were trying to keep the peace on the ground. By the time Christopher returned from Europe, support inside the administration for lift and strike had waned, and the plan was scrapped. In its place, the United States opted to continue to follow Europe's lead. By the end of May, the United States, Russia, Spain, the UK, and France agreed to a joint action plan to protect six safe areas in Bosnia, with force, if necessary; however, at this point, the United States had committed to providing only air support.[60]

For the following two years, the war in Bosnia continued, despite efforts from the UN and the European Community to negotiate a settlement. By the summer of 1995, Lake had given up on developing an interagency policy on Bosnia by acting as an honest broker in the process, shifting instead to the position of ardent policy advocate. He worked with members of his staff to take a strategic approach to solving the Bosnia problem rather than reacting to one crisis after another. Lake and his team developed an "end-game strategy," which called for the United States to take a decisive leadership role to resolve the war in Bosnia. It proposed a partition of the Bosnian state, with 51 percent of the land going to the Muslims and Croats and 49 percent to the Serbs. If a political settlement could not be reached, the end-game strategy called for the withdrawal of UN peacekeepers; the lifting of the arms embargo, with arms and training to be provided to the Croat and Muslim Bosnian forces; the enforcement of a no-fly zone; and

---

[60] Daalder (2000, pp. 17–19).

air strikes to defend safe areas. Before Lake brought his plan to the NSC/PC, he briefed it to the President and gained his support. Additionally, Lake asked President Clinton to visit the committee meeting at which Lake would present his plan to the rest of the principals and emphasize his desire for a long-term solution. At a July 17 NSC/PC meeting, Lake presented his strategy to the committee, receiving the expected reluctance from the other members, until the President joined them. The President told them that he had seen Lake's strategy but wanted to get everyone's input on a new plan for Bosnia. Effectively, Lake had kick-started the interagency process by going around it. Once the President made clear his interest in a significant break from past strategy, Lake returned to his role as honest broker in the interagency process. The Secretary of State and the Secretary of Defense each came up with separate plans, and, when presented to the President, the end-game strategy was chosen. It was the option with the best chance of resolving the situation in Bosnia once and for all, but it was also the one that posed the most risk to U.S. credibility and involved a significant commitment of the U.S. military to enforce a peace agreement.

Once the strategy was selected, Lake was chosen to take the plan to the European Community to get its support. Whereas Secretary Christopher had presented the lift-and-strike plan as an option for European consideration, Lake instead said that the United States had already decided what it was going to do and hoped that the Europeans would help. The Europeans, while not altogether pleased with every aspect of the end-game strategy, were relieved that the United States was willing to take the lead. With the allies on board, the next step was to conduct a diplomatic shuttle. Richard Holbrooke was chosen to lead the effort, and, while he and his team traveled throughout the Balkans, policy-makers in Washington worked through the details of an acceptable peace agreement. The NSC/PC had worked through plans for a new policy, but the plans for implementation were left to the NSC/DC.

In October 1995, the NSC/PC established an EXCOM whose purpose was to support Ambassador Holbrooke's negotiations and write a political-military plan for the implementation of a peace agreement. But a peace agreement did not exist yet, and its formulation was difficult and uncertain until the final day of the talks at Dayton. Holbrooke chose not to work with the EXCOM and instead dealt directly with the NSC/PC, rendering the EXCOM ineffective.[61] While Holbrooke was coordinating the agreement that was eventually concluded at a U.S. airbase in Dayton, Ohio, the NSC deputies in Washington began working on the implementation plan. Their meetings addressed three key issues: the mandate and mission of the NATO Implementation Force (IFOR), the exit strategy and deadline, and the civilian implementation effort.

The mission developed for IFOR was to enforce an agreed-upon peace settlement. This would be a unified NATO command with a UN mandate but no UN management role. It would have clear and robust rules of engagement and would focus on the military aspects of the peace agreement—marking boundaries, maintaining the separation of forces, and enforcing the cessation of hostilities. By the end of October, there were two, seemingly irreconcilable positions in Washington on the breadth of the IFOR mandate. The minimalists, led by National Security Advisor Lake, felt that the military's mission should be narrow, limited specifically to the military aspects of the agreement. The maximalists, led by Holbrooke, pushed for a broad mandate that would assign to the military such tasks as providing security during elections, arresting war criminals, protecting refugees returning to their homes, and responding to human-rights violations. This disagreement came to a head just before the negotiations in Dayton began. General Shalikashvili eventually devised the middle ground that could be accepted by both the minimalists and the maximalists. IFOR would be given the authority to assist in the civilian aspects of the implementation but would only be required to carry out the military aspects. This gave the commander of the force on the ground broad latitude to take on civil missions when the resources were available. It also paved the way for several years of squabbling between U.S. and NATO civilian and military leaders over who should be doing what,

---

[61] Institute for National Strategic Studies, National Defense University, *Improving the Utility of Presidential Decision Directive 56: A Plan of Action for the Joint Chiefs of Staff*, Washington, D.C., March 1999, pp. 8–9.

with the military seeking to limit civilian activities and the civilians seeking to expand them.

Once the issue of the mission was resolved in this manner, the overarching question in Washington was how long U.S. forces would be on the ground in Bosnia. Domestic political considerations led the deputies to agree to a one-year operation. The timeline specified by the Dayton accords called for all military aspects of the agreement to be fulfilled within 120 days. The basic goal of U.S. policy was to achieve a balance of power in Bosnia that would then secure peace and stability. The worst-case scenario was that, within a year, U.S. forces could build up Bosnian forces to even the military balance. Finally, it was believed that a balance of power and a year without fighting would create momentum for peace that would last after the withdrawal of NATO forces. This deadline took little account of the wider goals of the Dayton accords, which could not be achieved within a year, and was designed to keep Bosnia from becoming a major issue in the 1996 U.S. presidential election.

Once it became clear that the European Union would be appointing a high representative (HR) responsible for the civilian implementation to balance the U.S. command of the NATO force, Washington worked to diminish the power of the HR. Pauline Neville-Jones, the British negotiator at Dayton, said, "The U.S. negotiating tactic seemed to be to concede to this office as little authority as possible, either over the agencies engaged in civilian implementation or in relation to the military commander." She described the HR as "not fully answerable to any body of uncontested international authority and operates in uncomfortable and unconvincing limbo."[62] The HR was appointed by and overseen by the large and unwieldy Peace Implementation Council (PIC), the steering board consisting of representatives from the Group of Seven plus Russia. The civilian implementation organization is shown in Figure 4.1. It reflects the U.S. preference, which Washington would ultimately come to regret, to dilute European influence over that process by allocating important responsibilities to other organizations, such as democratization and elections to the Organization for

---

[62] Daalder (2000, pp. 156–157).

Figure 4.1
Civilian Implementation Organization in Bosnia

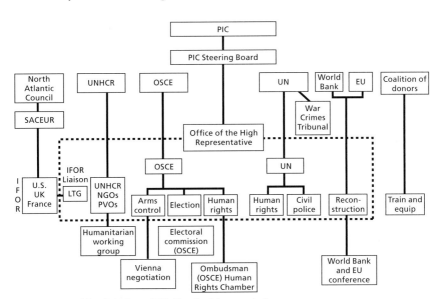

SOURCE: Daalder (2000, p. 158). Used with permission.
NOTE: SACEUR = Supreme Allied Commander Europe; UNHCR = UN High
Commissioner for Refugees.
RAND *MG716-4.1*

Security and Co-Operation in Europe (OSCE) and police reform to
the UN, rather than putting these under the EU's HR.

The General Framework Agreement for Peace, more widely
known as the Dayton accords, was initialed in Dayton on November
21 and signed in Paris on December 14, 1995. Under the accords, the
parties agreed to respect each other's sovereignty, settle disputes peace-
ably, respect human rights and the rights of refugees and displaced persons, and cooperate with all entities involved with implementing the
11 annexes addressing different aspects of the peace operation.[63] The
annexes were quite comprehensive and covered subjects as varied as
the cease-fire; cantonment of heavy weapons; the creation of an inter-

---

[63] Larry Wentz, ed., *Lessons from Bosnia: The IFOR Experience*, U.S. Department of
Defense Command and Control Research Program and National Defense University, 1997,
pp. 467–468.

national police task force; a new constitution; commissions on human rights, displaced persons, and refugees; and the preservation of national monuments.

Implementation

IFOR deployed on December 29, 1995. From November 1995 to February 1996, the Bosnia EXCOM proposed several plans for the civilian implementation, but the NSC/PC did not approve any of them. The inability to develop an integrated interagency plan reflected a fracture in the administration that went all the way to the cabinet. The main issue of contention continued to be how far IFOR would go to support the civilian implementation. This policy debate was not fully resolved for more than two years following the deployment of IFOR. With disagreements unresolved at the principals' level, the EXCOM continued to be ineffective.[64]

The policy debate that plagued the Bosnia operations focused on one fundamental question: Did the U.S. policy intend to end a war or build a peace? Initially, the minimalists won the battle of expectations in Washington, but, as international military efforts met with success, satisfaction with ending a war led to the realization that, to prevent its reccurrence, the focus must shift to building peace. IFOR could help guarantee an end to the fighting, but it would take a successful civilian implementation effort to build a lasting peace. However,

> [t]here was no formal integrating structure established at any level, and no means by which the military and civilian implementation plans and activities were reconciled and coordinated. The integration that did occur was primarily at the operational level—in Bosnia itself—and occurred as a result of *ad hoc* arrangements between the commander of IFOR/SFOR and the High Representative.[65]

---

[64] Institute for National Strategic Studies (1999, pp. 8–9).

[65] George A. Joulwan and Christopher C. Shoemaker, *Civilian-Military Cooperation in the Prevention of Deadly Conflict: Implementing the Agreements in Bosnia and Beyond*, New York: Carnegie Corporation, December 1995, p. 4. Italics in original.

Transition

IFOR's mission lasted only one year, as promised, but was replaced with the NATO Stabilization Force (SFOR), which represented, more or less, a change in name only. By March 1997, it was still behind schedule, and Ambassador Robert Gelbard led another planning effort to energize the process. This plan was approved up the channels of the U.S. government through the NSC/DC, NCS/PC, and the President, and it was used as a road map for the following year.[66]

At the end of SFOR's initial 18-month commitment, two and a half years after the first IFOR troops entered Bosnia, President Clinton announced that the United States would remain in Bosnia for as long as it would take for peace to become self-sustaining. An exit timeline would be replaced by clear benchmarks for self-sustaining peace, including a durable cease-fire; an effective police force; political, judicial, and economic reforms; the return of displaced persons; and cooperation with the international war-crimes tribunal. The Office of the High Representative was assigned increasing powers, gradually acquiring the ability to oversee all international civil activities in Bosnia, with the authority to impose legislation and replace obstructive local officials. NATO continued to reduce the size of SFOR in Bosnia as the security situation improved, and, in 2004, the European Union took over responsibility for peacekeeping in Bosnia, with a force of approximately 7,000.[67]

Presidential Decision Directive 56

Despite the long-term success of the NATO mission to Bosnia, there were significant shortfalls in interagency planning in Washington and coordination between military and civilian implementation authorities in Bosnia. Because of the regional organization of both DOS and DoD, many of those responsible for Bosnia had not participated in

---

[66] Institute for National Strategic Studies (1999, pp. 8–9).

[67] Julie Kim, *Bosnia: Overview of Issues Ten Years After Dayton*, CRS Report for Congress, Washington, D.C.: Congressional Research Service, November 14, 2005, p. 5.

planning for Haiti or Somalia, and many of the lessons from those experiences were not fully transmitted. In an attempt to institutionalize lessons drawn from such experiences for future use, PDD 56, Managing Complex Contingency Operations, was signed in May 1997. PDD 56 was developed to provide a basic doctrine for nation-building and to facilitate a unified U.S. government effort in such circumstances. To achieve this unity of effort, mechanisms were developed for the following decisionmaking requirements:

- Identify appropriate missions and tasks, if any, for U.S. government agencies in a U.S. government response.
- Develop strategies for early resolution of crises, thereby minimizing the loss of life and establishing the basis for reconciliation and reconstruction.
- Accelerate the planning and implementation of civilian aspects of the operation, and intensify action on critical funding and personnel requirements early on.
- Integrate all components of a U.S. response (e.g., civilian, military, police) at the policy level and facilitate the creation of coordination mechanisms at the operational level.
- Rapidly identify issues for senior policymakers and ensure the expeditious implementation of decisions.[68]

PDD 56 mandated six mechanisms to this end: an EXCOM, a political-military implementation plan, interagency political-military rehearsal, after-action review, training, and agency review and implementation.

The EXCOM had been marginalized in previous operations. PDD 56 sought to reiterate the need to have a standing interagency body to manage the day-to-day oversight of what were called *complex contingency operations*, the term *nation-building* having fallen out of fashion. The political-military implementation plan was to include a situation assessment, statement of U.S. interests, mission statement,

---

[68] White House, "The Clinton Administration's Policy on Managing Complex Contingency Operations: Presidential Decision Directive," white paper, May 1997.

list of key civil-military objectives, the desired political-military end state, concept of the operations, assignment of lead agency responsibilities, transition or exit strategy linked to the desired end state, the organizational concept, a list of any preparatory tasks, and a list of supporting plans. The process of developing the plan would help to ensure that agencies would not be working at cross-purposes and to minimize the gaps between agencies. The interagency political-military rehearsal would assist in synchronizing various elements of the plan. The after-action review would be conducted at the end of the operation and would formally capture lessons that could be used in the PDD 56–mandated agency training exercises and fed back into the planning process for the next operation. Finally, the lessons from the after-action review were to be assessed by each agency, and any required improvements would be implemented in an effort of continual process refinement and improvement. While some of the mechanisms of PDD 56 were never fully implemented, much of the directive was applied in the planning for Kosovo.

Kosovo

The disintegration of the former Yugoslavia continued in 1998, when violence erupted in Kosovo, a province of Serbia populated largely by ethnic Albanians but run, after Serbian President Slobodan Milosevic revoked its autonomous status in 1989, by Serbs. In February 1998, the Kosovo Liberation Army (KLA) began to challenge Serb security forces in a series of small-scale clashes. In July, the Serbs began a full-scale campaign against the KLA. This offensive in Kosovo aimed at sealing the border with Albania, minimizing the flow of support to the KLA, eliminating the KLA leadership, and pacifying the Kosovar Albanian population. The scorched-earth campaign resulted in extensive destruction of Kosovar villages and the displacement of 400,000 Kosovars.

Interagency Planning and the Decision to Intervene

In response to renewed violence in the Balkans, on August 11, 1998, the NSC/DC directed seven senior managers from the NSC staff, the Office of the Secretary of Defense, DOS, the CIA, and the Joint Staff "to develop a plan that would compel Slobodan Milosevic to cease his crackdown on the Kosovars."[69] The group was never designated an EXCOM, and it was staffed at the deputy assistant secretary level—one level lower than PDD 56 designated for an EXCOM. But the group acted as an interagency collaborative body tasked with developing a political-military plan. One member of the group had even helped to write PDD 56, so the EXCOM process was being used in practice, if not in name.[70]

The NSC/DC gave the group four weeks to develop its plan. In its first meeting, it developed a table of contents for the plan and split up the work. Although the plan did not follow the generic political-military plan format as laid out in PDD 56, all the subjects were covered. It started with purpose and intent, including policy questions for the NSC/DC. The second section of the plan was a strategic analysis of the situation in Kosovo. The third section discussed the relationship between force and diplomacy and addressed four key issues: keeping NATO united and engaged, keeping the Russians out of the game, keeping the issue out of the UNSC, and ensuring adequate maintenance of domestic support for any U.S. action.[71]

The fourth section covered advance preparations, the fifth addressed potential reactions from Belgrade, the sixth included Russia's reactions, the seventh concerned reactions from the rest of the world, the eighth reviewed humanitarian issues, the ninth covered human

---

[69] Steven P. Bucci, *Complex Contingencies: Presidential Decision Directive 56: The Case of Kosovo and the Future*, Arlington, Va.: National Foreign Affairs Training Center, undated, p. 20.

[70] Bucci (undated, p. 20).

[71] Bucci (undated, p. 21).

rights, and the tenth and last section reviewed postconflict requirements.[72] The plan became known as the presettlement plan.[73]

On September 4, the NSC/DC was briefed on the plan, which recommended bombing to get Milosevic to cease hostilities. Based on the anticipated consequences as laid out in the plan, the deputies decided against the bombing option at that time. Despite opting not to follow the interagency group's recommendation, the planning process was a success in that it facilitated an informed decision by the NSC/DC. When the plan was briefed to the NSC/PC, a senior policy manager described the ensuing discussion "as the highest level (in regard to quality) discussion he had ever seen conducted in 30 plus years of high government service. If the pol-mil plan's purpose was to inform the decision makers, it clearly did its job here."[74] It was decided that Richard Holbrooke would be sent on what became known as the October Mission to convince Milosevic to end his operations in Kosovo.

Holbrooke met with Milosevic for nine days and finally achieved an agreement that resolved what Ambassador Holbrooke characterized as "an emergency inside a crisis."[75] In other words, Milosevic had agreed to end the military campaign in Kosovo—the *emergency*—but there would be no resolution to the underlying political issues that led to the conflict—the *crisis*. The Holbrooke-Milosevic agreement had three major parts. First, Serb compliance would be monitored by a verification regime, which included overflights and international observers on the ground in Kosovo. Second, a U.S. diplomat, Christopher Hill, was identified as an international mediator. Finally, the Serbs agreed to a timetable to begin talks with the Kosovar Albanians. According to Daalder and O'Hanlon, the October mission had several limitations:

> First, for all the focus on verification, the details of what was to be verified . . . were left vague. Second, although the verifica-

---

[72] Bucci (undated, p. 22).

[73] Institute for National Strategic Studies, National Defense University (1999, p. 12).

[74] Bucci (undated, p. 22).

[75] Ivo H. Daalder and Michael E. O'Hanlon, *Winning Ugly: NATO's War to Save Kosovo*, Washington, D.C.: Brookings Institution Press, 2000, p. 49.

tion system set up in Kosovo was able to monitor Serb compliance, it was incapable of enforcing it. Indeed, the vulnerability of unarmed monitors operating in an area teeming with Serb forces seriously undermined NATO's ability to threaten or use force in case of Serb noncompliance. Third, in ignoring the Albanian side of the equation, the agreement offered no effective way to prevent the Kosovar Albanians from attempting to exploit the opening created by the retreat of Serb forces. . . . In this way, the agreement may have contained within it the seeds of its own demise.[76]

Now that an agreement had been reached, a plan had to be developed for what became the Kosovo Verification Mission (KVM). U.S. planning was conducted at U.S. European Command, with the assistance of a senior manager from the Office of the Secretary of Defense and representatives from DOS and the CIA. Since the KVM was to be carried out by OSCE, the U.S.-developed plan did not contain much detail and was presented to both OSCE and the UN as a "concept brief."[77] This concept brief became the basis for the mission that was deployed to Kosovo.

At the same time as the KVM plan was being developed, DOS officials chaired an interagency planning team charged with developing a postsettlement implementation plan. Working from the Haiti experience, they integrated military and civil tasks, such as public security, elections, and reconstruction, to implement a peace agreement. Despite its momentum, this planning effort never had the backing of any agency leaders or high-level interagency group and finally shut down in January 1999.[78] No one knew what steps the United States and NATO were willing to take to create or enforce a peace agreement in November and December, and the situation remained uncertain.

Secretary of State Albright never believed that Milosevic would uphold his side of any agreement unless NATO proved that it was willing to use force. Albright thought the agreement was failing and

---

[76] Daalder and O'Hanlon (2000, p. 50).

[77] Bucci (undated, p. 24).

[78] Institute for National Strategic Studies, National Defense University (1999, p. 12).

wanted to target Milosevic with direct pressure. She had her spokes-person, James Rubin, tell the press, "Milosevic has been at the center of every crisis in the former Yugoslavia over the last decade. He is not simply part of the problem; Milosevic is the problem."[79] In December, KVM head, U.S. Ambassador William Walker, said that "both sides have been looking for trouble and they have found it. If the two sides are unwilling to live up to their agreements, 2,000, 3,000, or 4,000 unarmed verifiers cannot frustrate their attempts to go after each other."[80] No one in Washington, except Secretary Albright, was ready to give up on the Holbrooke-Milosevic agreement yet.

On January 15, 1999, the NSC/PC met to discuss a 13-page Kosovo strategy paper known as "October-Plus." It proposed strengthening the KVM with more personnel, helicopters, and bodyguards; training an Albanian police force; and preparing for summer elections in Kosovo. The goal of the October-Plus strategy was "to promote regional stability and protect our investment in Bosnia; prevent the resumption of hostilities in Kosovo and renewed humanitarian crisis; [and] preserve U.S. and NATO credibility."[81] Albright came to the meeting prepared to offer other options.

> She noted that the October agreement was about to fall apart. . . . Hill's negotiation efforts were stymied by Serb obstruction-ism and Albanian fragmentation. The administration now faced a "decision point." It had three options: "stepping back, muddling through, or taking decisive steps." As violence escalated and a new humanitarian crisis loomed, stepping back was not a real option. As for muddling through, at best it might postpone the inevitable collapse of the October agreement; at worst it amounted to what one senior NATO official termed "a strategy of incrementally reinforcing failure." That left decisive steps. . . . [S]he emphasized that "Milosevic needed to realize that he faced a real potential for

---

[79] Daalder and O'Hanlon (2000, p. 69).

[80] Daalder and O'Hanlon (2000, pp. 61–62).

[81] Daalder and O'Hanlon (2000, p. 70).

NATO action. If he did not get that message, he would not make any concessions."[82]

The principals chose the October-Plus option. After the meeting, Albright was quoted as saying, "We're just gerbils running on a wheel."[83] The PDD 56 process was not being used, and, at this point, the planning for Kosovo resembled the planning that had occurred in response to Bosnia.

The NSC/PC would not be satisfied by this decision for long. Shortly after adjourning from the January 15 meeting, the Racak massacre was reported. Within hours, Jim Steinberg convened a meeting of the NSC/DC with representatives from DOS, DoD, the JCS, and the CIA. DOS argued for immediate air strikes, and DoD asked, What would be the objective? The group met for several days and made no decisions. Meanwhile, Secretary Albright and her staff were working on a new strategy. Using input from Alexander Vershbow, the U.S. ambassador to NATO, Albright put new proposals to an NSC/PC meeting on January 19.

> Albright's strategy consisted of an ultimatum to the parties to accept an interim settlement by a date certain. If the parties accepted the deal, NATO would commit to its enforcement with troops on the ground. However, if Belgrade refused to endorse the plan, NATO's standing orders to its military commanders to commence a phased air campaign would be implemented. Albright was explicit about the strategy's key assumptions. First, since the allies would not deploy their troops on their own for fear of having to repeat the disaster of Bosnia, American troops would have to be part of any international force. Second, Milosevic would never accept the need to negotiate seriously, let alone accept an interim settlement, if there was no credible bombing threat. Third, further negotiations would lead nowhere; therefore,

---

[82] Daalder and O'Hanlon (2000, p. 70).

[83] Daalder and O'Hanlon (2000, p. 71).

an interim deal had to be imposed through the threat and, if necessary, the use of NATO airpower.[84]

On January 20, President Clinton approved Secretary Albright's plan, which laid the foundation for the peace conference at Rambouillet. Once again, as he had done with Tony Lake's end-game strategy in Bosnia, President Clinton chose an option presented by one of his principal advisers instead of a plan developed in an interagency forum.

The Rambouillet conference opened on February 6, and was soon being called "Château Dayton."[85] The proposed agreement resembled, in some respects, the Dayton accords. The draft began with a brief framework agreement and was followed by a series of annexes addressing such issues as a constitution for Kosovo, elections, and military and civilian implementation.[86] According to Timothy Garton Ash,

> First, while all Western participants entered the talks in the hope of reaching an agreement, the U.S., and specifically the State Department, had a much clearer fallback position than its European allies. This position was, as Albright herself subsequently put it, to achieve, "clarity." If the Kosovar Albanians signed, and the Serbs did not, then even the most hesitant European ally (and the Congress, and the White House) must surely be convinced of the need to bomb Milosevic into accepting autonomy for Kosovo.[87]

The talks continued through March 18, when the Kosovar Albanians were finally persuaded to sign the agreement. When the Serbs refused, the conference was adjourned, and six days later, on March 24, Operation Allied Force, the air war over Kosovo, began.

---

[84] Daalder and O'Hanlon (2000, pp. 71–72).

[85] Timothy Garton Ash, "Kosovo: Was It Worth It?" *New York Review of Books*, Vol. 47, No. 14, September 21, 2000.

[86] Daalder and O'Hanlon (2000, p. 78).

[87] Ash (2000).

Implementation

The September presettlement plan, which had recommended a bombing campaign, was taken off the shelf, and the NSC/DC began day-to-day oversight of the operation as NATO entered its first war.

> EXCOM duties were for all intents and purposes sucked upwards to the Deputies Committee. The entire issue became so high profile, that it became a nearly daily agenda for them. The added crush of time, and the full internationalization of the crisis . . . skewed the process away from any semblance of systemization.[88]

Everyone expected the air war to last two or three days. General Michael Short, the commander of the allied air forces, said,

> I can't tell you how many times the instruction I got was, "Mike, you're only going to be allowed to bomb two, maybe three nights. That's all Washington can stand. That's all some members of the alliance can stand. That's why you've only got 90 targets. This'll be over in three nights."

NATO's commander of southern forces, Admiral James Ellis, agreed: "We called this one *absolutely* wrong."[89]

Another mistake that was made at the outset of the air campaign was a vast underestimation of the number of refugees that could be expected. NATO intelligence had predicted 200,000 refugees. By the end of April, there were 850,000 refugees and internally displaced persons.[90] A foreshadowing of Operation Horseshoe, the ethnic cleansing of Kosovar Albanians, can be found in a January conversation between Milosevic and General Wesley Clark. Milosevic told Clark,

> You know, General Clark, that we know how to handle these Albanians, these murderers, these rapists, these killers-of-their-own-kind. We have taken care of them before. In Drenica, in

---

[88] Bucci (undated, p. 27).

[89] Ash (2000).

[90] Ash (2000).

1946, we killed them. We killed them all. Oh, it took several years, but we eventually killed them all.[91]

The military campaign in Kosovo was constrained by political considerations, both domestic and international. President Clinton limited his options from the beginning by publicly declaring that there would be no ground campaign, a pledge he came to regret. There were still tensions between DOS, which came to favor a ground offensive, and DoD, which opposed it. General Wesley Clark, the top U.S. and NATO commander in Europe (who favored the DOS view) described it as "a grudge match that went back to Bosnia."[92] All this occurred under the immense pressure of maintaining a fragile 19-nation NATO alliance. In the end, the administration got the balance between diplomacy and force just right, forcing a Serb capitulation without suffering a single casualty, but the process occasioned much wrangling and considerable uncertainty.

Once it became clear that the bombing campaign might last more than a few days, the NSC/DC, in late March, tasked the Kosovo EXCOM to prepare a political-military plan for peace implementation after the bombing campaign ended.[93] In the first week of April, 30 experts and planners from 18 agencies formed an interagency working group. They quickly identified 14 mission areas: governance, military, refugee repatriation, humanitarian relief, demining, police, elections, democratization, administration of criminal justice, human rights, war crimes, international public information, financial matters, and reconstruction.[94] The group met at least twice weekly and issued various position papers, which formed a consolidated mission analysis. "A

[91] Wesley K. Clark, *Waging Modern War: Bosnia, Kosovo, and the Future of Combat*, New York: Public Affairs, 2001, pp. 151–152.

[92] Michael Ignatieff, "Chains of Command," *New York Review of Books*, Vol. 48, No. 12, July 19, 2001, p. 17.

[93] Richard Roan, Erik Kjonnerod, and Robert Oakley, "Dealing with Complex Contingencies," Institute for National Strategic Studies Transition Papers, Washington, D.C.: National Defense University, December 21, 2000, pp. 4–6.

[94] National Security Council Deputies Committee, *Mission Analysis: International Provisional Administration (IPA) for Kosovo*, draft staff assessment, 1999, p. 6.

network of interlocking working groups sweated the details the [U.S. government] could pin down as State awaited diplomatic action which would define the 'super-structure'—lead organizations, an actual UN mandate—and, of course compliance with NATO's conditions."[95]

By mid-May, a final product called the Kosovo Mission Analysis was approved by the NSC/DC. This document, which was not called a political-military plan so that it would encounter less resistance in the international community, laid out the basic principles of the relationship between the prospective UN Mission in Kosovo (UNMIK) and the NATO Kosovo Force (KFOR) as it ultimately appeared in UNSC Resolution 1244, which formally ended the conflict.[96] It also set the foundation for the four pillars of the civilian implementation effort: humanitarian support, governance support, institutional development, and reconstruction. Human rights were seen as a part of each of the four pillars, and the need to deploy an international police force was also acknowledged.[97]

While the PDD 56 process was sporadically applied until March 1999, once it was fully invoked after the start of the air campaign to plan for the eventual peace, it was successful. "The interagency coordination and planning effort that produced the Kosovo Mission Analysis was a flexible and highly effective implementation of the coordination mechanisms and planning tools of PDD 56."[98] However, PDD 56 was only partially implemented. The Kosovo mission analysis did not follow the format of the PDD 56 generic political-military plan, but it included all the pertinent information. Critical to the success of the interagency effort was the oversight of the NSC/DC. The deputies' participation ensured that the relevant agencies participated fully in the process and "ensured accountability and coordination by involved

---

[95] David Newsom, "Background Press Brief on Kosovo IPA," U.S. Department of State, June 11, 1999.

[96] See UNSC Resolution 1244, on the situation in Kosovo, June 10, 1999.

[97] Newsom (1999).

[98] Roan, Kjonnerod, and Oakley (2000, p. 5).

agencies during the implementation phase."[99] In April, the U.S. Congress passed a supplemental bill that provided adequate funding for the peace-implementation operation. The comprehensive mission analysis is also credited with helping the administration to secure this financial support from the Congress.

The overall mission of the international provisional administration (IPA) for Kosovo, as described in the mission analysis, was as follows: "The IPA will provide transitional administration while establishing and overseeing the development of provisional democratic self-governing institutions to ensure conditions for a peaceful and normal life for all inhabitants of Kosovo."[100] The operational requirements for the IPA included "rapid and early deployment," "maximum authority, flexibility, and political/legal legitimacy," and a seamless interface with KFOR.[101] On June 10, UNSC Resolution 1244 was passed, and on June 12, KFOR and UNMIK deployed into Kosovo, where they remain as of this writing, albeit in much reduced numbers.

Conclusion

Through the four responses to humanitarian crises and ethnic wars in the 1990s, the U.S. government learned a multitude of lessons, some valid, a few pernicious. When it came time to plan the Kosovo intervention, the Clinton administration had largely abandoned its post-Somalia fixation on limiting "mission creep," establishing exit strategies, and setting departure deadlines. The UNSC resolution that set up the Kosovo mission made clear that the NATO military would assume responsibility for policing and public order until the UN could deploy enough international civilian police to assume these functions. The mandates for the NATO and UN missions were open ended and remain in effect more than eight years later.

---

[99] Roan, Kjonnerod, and Oakley (2000, p. 6).

[100] National Security Council Deputies Committee (1999, p. 1).

[101] National Security Council Deputies Committee (1999, p. 2).

Perhaps the most important lesson drawn by the Clinton administration from these experiences was the need for integrated political-military planning, developed through interagency coordination, which would be the keystone of a comprehensive U.S. response. In the wake of the National Defense University after-action review of Haiti, doctrine for interagency collaboration in the management of complex contingency operations was finally codified in PDD 56. By the time the United States was gearing up for intervention in Kosovo, key players recognized that policy development and detailed interagency planning did not equate to a case of the chicken or the egg. Each process informed the other, and policy development and interagency planning were undertaken as iterative, with several plans drafted to adjust to changing U.S. policies and realities on the ground. Detailed interagency planning was a way to clearly define assumptions, posit likely outcomes, and identify the costs of intervening. Understanding these led to better policy development and decisionmaking at the highest levels of government. Additional lessons included the need for periodic policy review, especially during implementation, when the nature of events in theater may change; the need for an interagency training program to allow planners to better understand the interagency process and the capabilities and limitations of the different agencies that make up the interagency environment; a need for a cadre of planners across the U.S. government ready to respond to future crises; and, finally, a need for interagency coordination at all levels of the mission—from strategic to tactical. Unfortunately, most of these lessons would have to be relearned, at some considerable cost, by the successor administration of George W. Bush.

CHAPTER FIVE

Post-9/11 Nation-Building: Afghanistan and Iraq

George W. Bush ran for president on a platform that clearly opposed heavy U.S. involvement in nation-building. With the September 11, 2001, attacks on New York and Washington, D.C., the U.S. view of the post–Cold War order changed dramatically, and with it, albeit more slowly, so did President Bush's attitude toward such missions.

Most on the Bush team had observed the spate of post–Cold War missions from the sidelines and drawn lessons that were at odds with the practices that evolved during the Clinton administration. Following the debacle of Somalia, the disappointing results of his intervention in Haiti, and the slow progress in Bosnia, Clinton had reluctantly abandoned the search for quick exit strategies. In carrying out subsequent nation-building operations, his administration had employed overwhelming force, sought the broadest possible multilateral participation in all its efforts, and eventually accepted the need for long-term commitment to societies that it was trying to reform and rebuild. By contrast, even when faced with the need, first in Afghanistan and then in Iraq, to engage in very large-scale nation-building enterprises, the Bush administration remained wary of long-term entanglements, emphasized economy of force, was skeptical of multilateral institutions, and envisaged a quite limited role for the United States in rebuilding these societies.

The President and His Administration

In terms of personal style, George W. Bush was more outgoing and charismatic than his father but lacked the elder Bush's bureaucratic, legislative, and foreign-policy experience. The younger Bush was generally goal-oriented in his approach to policy, preferring to delegate details to trusted subordinates. His cabinet and staff resembled those of former presidents, such as Truman and Clinton, in that it mixed experienced and forceful Washington insiders, such as Colin Powell and Donald Rumsfeld, with associates from his time in Texas politics. His cabinet, particularly in his first term, would be the scene of clashes among many of these officials, which the President allowed, up to a point. Bush's cognitive style can thus be characterized by a preference for focusing on themes rather than details. He had confidence in his own efficacy as a manager and leader and a modest tolerance for conflict while placing the highest premium on loyalty.

The structure of the NSC under George W. Bush was similar to those of the George H. W. Bush and Clinton administrations before him. National Security Presidential Directive (NSPD) 1 describes the composition and responsibilities of the NSC, the NSC/PC, the NSC/DC, and the policy coordination committees along familiar lines. The U.S. representative to the United Nations was no longer listed as a member of the NSC.[1] A significant addition to the structure of the George W. Bush administration instituted by NSPD 1 is that the Vice President would chair NSC meetings in the absence of the President.

The NSC/PC was similar to those of the previous two administrations, consisting of the Assistant to the President for National Security Affairs (as the chair), the Deputy National Security Advisor, the Secretary of State, the Secretary of Defense, and the President's Chief of Staff. The Secretary of the Treasury was made a regular member of the NSC/PC. However, the Director of Central Intelligence and the Chair of the JCS moved from being regular members to the NSC/PC to attending when necessary. Both the Vice President's Chief of Staff and

---

[1]   George W. Bush, National Security Presidential Directive 1, Organization of the National Security Council System, Washington, D.C.: White House, February 13, 2001.

National Security Advisor had seats on this committee.[2] Conversely, in the George H. W. Bush administration, the Vice President had no representation on NSC committees, and the Clinton administration had only one representative.

The NSC/DC was also largely similar to those from the previous two administrations. Regular members of the NSC/DC, which is chaired by the Deputy National Security Advisor, include the Deputy Secretary of State, Under Secretary of the Treasury, or Under Secretary of the Treasury for International Affairs; the Deputy Secretary of Defense or Under Secretary of Defense for Policy; the Deputy Director of Central Intelligence; the Vice Chair of the JCS, the Vice President's National Security Advisor; and the President's Deputy Assistant for International Economic Affairs. Again, the Office of the Vice President had two, rather than one, seats on this committee.[3]

Under the George W. Bush administration, Clinton administration NSC IWGs replaced policy coordination committees. NSPD 1 formed six regional committees and 11 functional working groups.[4] None of these played an important role in coordinating policy toward Afghanistan or Iraq.

Early in the Bush administration, an NSPD was drafted to replace PDD 56. This draft proposed to build on the Clinton structure in a number of constructive ways, including new provisions for contingency warning, advanced planning, prevention, and the development of response options. It established the Contingency Planning Policy Coordinating Committee, whose purpose was to develop "interagency contingency plans for emerging crises with a focus on U.S. objectives, a desired end state, policy options, interagency responsibilities, resource issues, and strategies for various aspects of the operation." It also required an interagency training program "to develop a cadre of professionals capable of planning for complex contingency operations."

---

[2] G. W. Bush (2001).

[3] G. W. Bush (2001).

[4] G. W. Bush (2001).

NSPD "XX" also required a quarterly NSC/DC review to determine whether planning for contingencies should begin.[5]

Although the draft NSPD provided a "comprehensive framework for organizing the interagency nation-building process," it was never issued.[6] The Pentagon blocked the document "in the name of preserving the freedom of action of Cabinet officers and keeping civilians out of the contingency planning business."[7] As a result, most of the process lessons that had been developed in the wake of the Clinton administration's experiences in Somalia, Haiti, and Bosnia were jettisoned. When it came time for planning for Afghanistan and Iraq, none of the procedures laid out in the draft NSPD was followed.

Several factors probably contributed to this rejection. New administrations are often reluctant to simply pick up where their predecessors left off. Second, Condoleezza Rice entered office espousing a more limited role for the NSC than did some of her predecessors. She cut the staff size, shed some functions, and saw her role primarily as an adviser to the President, rather as the conductor of an interagency orchestra. Finally, Secretary of Defense Donald Rumsfeld took his prerogatives for the command and control of U.S. military forces very seriously, informing Rice pointedly on one occasion that she was not part of the chain of command.

This military chain of command formally runs from the President to the Secretary of Defense to the theater military commanders. It thus also bypasses the Chair of the JCS, despite that officer's nominal role as the President's senior military adviser. In practice, however, the national security adviser and staff had inserted themselves into the process of directing U.S. military operations in several ways during the previous several decades, becoming the core of what Pentagon doc-

---

[5]   Michèle Flournoy, "Interagency Strategy and Planning for Post-Conflict Reconstruction," in Robert C. Orr, ed., *Winning the Peace: An American Strategy for Post-Conflict Reconstruction*, Washington, D.C.: CSIS Press, 2004, pp. 107, 112.

[6]   Francis Fukuyama, "Introduction: Nation-Building and the Failure of Institutional Memory," in Francis Fukuyama, ed., *Nation-Building: Beyond Afghanistan and Iraq*, Baltimore, Md.: Johns Hopkins University Press, 2006, p. 8.

[7]   Joseph J. Collins, "Planning Lessons from Afghanistan and Iraq," *Joint Forces Quarterly*, No. 41, 2nd quarter, 2006, p. 12.

uments describe, somewhat vaguely, as the "national command authority." In successfully suppressing NSPD XX, Rumsfeld sought to restrict such involvement and minimize oversight of DoD activities by White House staffers.

Five years into the Bush administration, in December of 2005, NSPD 44, Management of Interagency Efforts Concerning Reconstruction and Stabilization, was signed. NSPD 44 was specifically written as a replacement for PDD 56. It focused on the civilian side of nation-building, with limited discussion of coordination between DOS and DoD, calling for the integration of

> stabilization and reconstruction contingency plans with military contingency plans when relevant and appropriate. The Secretaries of State and Defense will develop a general framework for fully coordinating stabilization and reconstruction activities and military operations at all levels where appropriate.[8]

Considerably less expansive and prescriptive than NSPD XX, it nevertheless sought to restore some of the mechanisms developed during the Clinton administration for handling such contingencies.

The collegial environment that marked the NSC of the first Bush and the Clinton administrations was lacking in the younger Bush's administration. This was due, in part, to the heavyweight set of personalities Bush had recruited to counterbalance his own lack of experience. Besides Vice President Dick Cheney, Secretary of Defense Donald Rumsfeld, Secretary of State Colin Powell, Deputy Secretary of State Richard Armitage, and Deputy Secretary of Defense Paul Wolfowitz not only possessed immense executive-branch experience, they were also highly motivated, strong personalities. All were older and more experienced than Condoleezza Rice, whose only government experience had been as a junior NSC staffer a decade earlier.

This team proved to be difficult to orchestrate, as many participants would simply act unilaterally when so inclined. President Bush

---

8 George W. Bush, National Security Presidential Directive 44, Management of Interagency Efforts Concerning Reconstruction and Stabilization, Washington, D.C.: White House, December 7, 2005.

conceived of himself as a strong manager, but it would have required considerable effort and great familiarity with the details of policy and the ways of the federal bureaucracy to personally monitor and control the activity of his subordinates. The President failed to make that effort, and he did not empower his staff to do so on his behalf. As a result, according to one observer, his "National Security Council was a system that assumed senior officials would cooperate and share information with their counterparts and which rarely cracked down when they did not."[9]

Afghanistan

Planning for the Postwar Period

In response to the September 11 attacks, the United States gave the Taliban—the ruling government in Afghanistan—the opportunity to turn over members of the al Qaeda organization. The Taliban refused, and regime change in Afghanistan quickly became the goal of the United States. However, there were no standing contingency plans for action in Afghanistan. In the weeks following, a military plan was quickly developed that relied primarily on covert CIA operatives, military special forces, and U.S. airpower, with the majority of the "boots on the ground" being provided by the Northern Alliance, a loose confederation of militias in opposition to the Taliban. The question of what would come after the Taliban had not been addressed before the war started. Strong pressure to respond quickly to the September 11 attacks and an unwillingness—and, logistically, an inability—to put a large number of U.S. forces on the ground in Afghanistan combined to define and constrain U.S. planning.

U.S. Central Command (USCENTCOM) developed the military plan for Afghanistan. Its three objectives were to destroy al Qaeda in Afghanistan, remove the ruling Taliban regime, and help the Afghan people through the rebuilding of infrastructure and hospitals and the

---

[9]   Michael R. Gordon and General Bernard E. Trainor, *Cobra II: The Inside Story of the Invasion and Occupation of Iraq*, New York: Pantheon Books, 2006, p. 148.

provision of humanitarian aid.[10] USCENTCOM's plan for the post-conflict phase, phase IV, was titled, significantly, Establish Capacity of Coalition Partners to Prevent the Re-Emergence of Terrorism and Provide Support for Humanitarian Assistance Efforts.[11] The United States did not intend to take upon itself the job of nation-building in Afghanistan. At an October 12, 2001, NSC meeting, President Bush said that he was against "using the military for nation-building. Once the job is done, our forces are not peacekeepers. We ought to put in place a U.N. protection and leave."[12]

The NSC and the NSC/PC gathered daily in September and October to discuss the war in Afghanistan and the response to 9/11, but no grand strategy was developed. Secretary of State Colin Powell characterized the effort as developing a response, but not a strategy. Bob Woodward wrote that it was "Powell's worst nightmare—bomb and hope."[13] There was little interest at the highest levels of the U.S. government to get into postwar planning. In response to a question about what the United States would do after the fall of the Taliban, Secretary of Defense Rumsfeld said at a press conference,

> I don't think [it] leaves us with a responsibility to try to figure out what kind of government that country ought to have. I don't know people who are smart enough to tell other countries the kind of arrangements they ought to have to govern themselves.[14]

On October 12, President Bush expressed the desire to turn the post-Taliban administration of Afghanistan over to the UN. Powell suggested a UN mandate with other military forces, neither U.S. nor

---

[10] Michael DeLong and Noah Lukeman, *Inside CENTCOM: the Unvarnished Truth About the Wars in Afghanistan and Iraq*, Washington, D.C.: Regnery Publishing, 2004, p. 36.

[11] Tommy Franks with Malcolm McConnell, *American Soldier*, New York: Regan Books, 2004, pp. 271–272.

[12] Bob Woodward, *Bush at War*, New York: Simon and Schuster, 2002, p. 237.

[13] Woodward (2002, pp. 174–175).

[14] Woodward (2002, p. 220).

Northern Alliance, providing security in Kabul.[15] At an October 15 NSC meeting, President Bush said, "There's been too much discussion of post conflict Afghanistan. We've been at it for a week. We've made a lot of progress, we've got time."[16]

Despite the lack of interest among the NSC principals in getting into postwar planning, the NSC/DC did provide some integration of effort across the government for a response to postconflict, post-Taliban Afghanistan, meeting on October 3 to discuss this topic. The deputies agreed that "the United States should lead the efforts to stabilize post-Taliban Afghanistan, including helping with food production, health, education for women, small-scale infrastructure projects and clearing the country of land mines." They also saw the need for developing plans for political structure, security, public information, encouraging international donors, and setting up an international conference on Afghanistan's political future.[17] However, in the absence of a PDD 56–like framework for planning, much of the resultant work was ad hoc; no working group was created, no integrated civil-military plan was developed, and no senior coordinator was named to head such an effort.[18] In the absence of a grand strategy or integrated political-military plan, the way the war unfolded on the ground in Afghanistan drove the nature of the U.S. involvement in postwar planning.

On November 13, 2002, the Northern Alliance entered Kabul, effectively marking the end of the Taliban regime.[19] Negotiations on the future of the government of Afghanistan would have to reflect the realities that the Northern Alliance and the various warlords who made up that loose federation were now in a position of power.[20] The Tajik and Uzbek leaders of the Northern Alliance began moving back into

---

[15] Woodward (2002, p. 231).

[16] Woodward (2002, p. 241).

[17] Woodward (2002, p. 193).

[18] Flournoy (2004, p. 107).

[19] Woodward (2002, p. 310).

[20] Milan Vaishnav, "Afghanistan: The Chimera of the 'Light Footprint,'" in Robert C. Orr, ed., *Winning the Peace: An American Strategy for Post-Conflict Reconstruction*, Washington, D.C.: CSIS Press, 2004, p. 248.

the presidential palace and various ministries in Kabul from which many of them had been driven by the Taliban half a decade earlier.[21] Under U.S. and international pressure, the Northern Alliance leadership was persuaded to join with other, mostly Pashtun émigré elements of the opposition to form a more broadly based government. At a UN-chaired conference in Bonn, Germany, a Pashtun, Hamid Karzai, was chosen to head this provisional administration. Karzai took office on December 22, 2001, with backing from the U.S. government, a largely united international community, and all the principal Northern Alliance military commanders. The Bonn conference had also requested the deployment of an international military force, though the United States successfully insisted that its initial activities should not extend beyond the capital, Kabul.

During the succeeding months, the U.S. military continued to focus on chasing down the fleeing remnants of al Qaeda and the Taliban while assuming no responsibility for establishing public security. To make the terrorist-hunting easier, the United States opposed expanding NATO's International Security Assistance Force (ISAF) beyond Kabul, lest its activities bring it into conflict with the local militia commanders who were helping in these antiterrorist efforts. The U.S. military did successfully use its influence to prevent a resumption of large-scale fighting among various regional commanders, but such security for the civilian population outside Kabul continued to rest with local militias.

Allies

On November 14, 2001, UNSC Resolution 1378 called for the UN to play a "central role" in "establishing a transitional administration and inviting member states to send peacekeeping forces to promote stability and aid delivery."[22] After the fall of Kabul, the major Afghan factions

---

[21] S. Frederick Starr, "Sovereignty and Legitimacy in Afghan Nation-Building" in Francis Fukuyama, ed., *Nation-Building: Beyond Afghanistan and Iraq*, Baltimore, Md.: Johns Hopkins University Press, 2006, p. 111.

[22] Kenneth Katzman, *Afghanistan: Post-War Governance, Security, and U.S. Policy*, CRS Report for Congress, Washington, D.C.: Congressional Research Service, November 3,

signed the Bonn Agreement on December 5, 2001, at the UN-hosted conference. It was endorsed by UNSC Resolution 1383 on December 6, 2001.[23] Iran, Russia, India, and Pakistan, the principal external sponsors of Afghanistan's long-running civil war, participated in the Bonn conference. The first three cooperated closely with the United States in forging the outcome, Iran playing a particularly constructive role. Pakistan was unenthusiastic about the demise of its client, the Taliban, but endorsed, somewhat reluctantly, the successor regime.

The Bonn Agreement established an interim administration with Hamid Karzai at the head and laid out a process for development of a constitution and national elections. It also requested that an international force with a UN mandate be dispatched to provide security in Kabul. UNSC Resolution 1401 established the United Nations Assistance Mission in Afghanistan (UNAMA), whose purpose was to assist in the implementation of the Bonn Agreement.[24] Lakhdar Brahimi, who had chaired the Bonn conference, was put in charge of UNAMA.

The 5,000-strong ISAF began to deploy to Kabul in December. It operated under British national, not UN, control. At this point, neither the United States nor the UN wished to take on the responsibility for securing Afghanistan. The UN felt that the task was too demanding for lightly armed UN peacekeepers. The United States preferred to leave Afghan security to the Afghans, though the country lacked both an army and a police force. The UN confined its activities largely to the political sphere, skillfully overseeing the constitutional processes laid out in the Bonn accords. For the next 18 months, ISAF, under a succession of national commands, functioned independently of the UN, NATO, and the U.S.-led coalition.

In early 2002, Colin Powell, responding to pleas from Karzai and Brahimi, urged that ISAF peacekeeping be extended beyond Kabul to the country's other main population centers. The issue was discussed

---

2006, p. 7. See also UNSC Resolution 1378, on the situation in Afghanistan, November 14, 2001.

[23] UNSC Resolution 1383, on the situation in Afghanistan, December 6, 2001.

[24] Vaishnav (2004, p. 253). See also UNSC Resolution 1401, on the situation in Afghanistan, March 28, 2002.

at an NSC/PC meeting at which Rumsfeld successfully opposed the extension, offering instead to instruct U.S. commanders in Afghanistan to use their influence with local militia commanders to tamp down any resumption of large-scale civil conflict.

Responsibility for rebuilding the Afghan army, police, courts, and other governmental institutions was divvied up among a number of donors, with the United States taking the lead with the army, Germany with the police, Italy with the courts, the UK with the counternarcotics effort, and the World Bank with the economy. Various committees were established to coordinate these efforts, but no individual, country, or international organization was assigned responsibility for integrating these national and sectoral efforts into an overall strategy.[25]

On January 21, 2002, Japan hosted the International Conference on Reconstruction Assistance to Afghanistan in Tokyo.[26] Donors pledged $5.2 billion over five years to assist in the rebuilding of Afghanistan, of which the U.S. share was an uncharacteristically low 10 percent. A joint team of the Asian Development Bank, the UN Development Programme, and the World Bank assessed that Afghanistan would need at least $10.2 billion in the first five years of reconstruction.

Throughout 2002, U.S. economic assistance to Afghanistan amounted to some $500 million, or about $20 per Afghan. Other international assistance was not much greater, bringing the total to only $50 per inhabitant. It is likely that most of this money was spent on overhead and foreign advisers, so the average Afghan received even less.[27]

---

[25] Larry P. Goodson, "The Lessons of Nation-Building in Afghanistan," in Francis Fukuyama, ed., *Nation-Building: Beyond Afghanistan and Iraq*, Baltimore, Md.: Johns Hopkins University Press, 2006, p. 149.

[26] Olga Oliker, Richard Kauzlarich, James Dobbins, Kurt W. Basseuner, Donald L. Sampler, John G. McGinn, Michael J. Dziedzic, Adam Grissom, Bruce L. Pirnie, Nora Bensahel, and A. Isar Guven, *Aid During Conflict: Interaction Between Military and Civilian Assistance Providers in Afghanistan, September 2001–June 2002*, Santa Monica, Calif.: RAND Corporation, MG-212-OSD, 2004, p. 78.

[27] By contrast, international assistance to Bosnia amounted to $800 per inhabitant in the first year after that war.

U.S. and international military force levels were also exceptionally thin on the ground, consistent with the administration's desire to
maintain a small footprint. Some 10,000 U.S. soldiers were deployed
in 2002, along with the 5,000 international troops deployed as part
of ISAF. By contrast, NATO had sent 60,000 soldiers into Bosnia in
1996 and nearly 50,000 into Kosovo in 1999, for a total of more than
100,000 soldiers to pacify two societies that were, combined, five times
less populous than Afghanistan.

In August 2003, NATO assumed command of ISAF, ending a
succession of six-month turnovers in independent national command.
In October of that year, UNSC Resolution 1510 lifted the Kabul-only
restriction on ISAF, authorizing its expansion beyond the capital.[28] The
actual expansion took place gradually over the following two years.
It was only in October 2006 that the NATO-led ISAF became the
lead international security force in Afghanistan, though a large, independent U.S.-led coalition continued to conduct counterterrorism and
training activities.[29]

Implementation

With the installation of a new Afghan administration, the United
States had no formal responsibility for governing Afghanistan but was
given great leeway by the fledgling government to carry out military
operations throughout the country, hunting the remnants of the Taliban and al Qaeda. The reach of ISAF and the central government was
initially limited to a small area surrounding the capital, with the rest of
the nation controlled by local warlords, tribal chiefs, and militia commanders. With the U.S. focus largely on hunting terrorists, scant U.S.
resources were unavailable for other priorities. The first U.S. ambassador to Afghanistan, Robert Finn, lacked the personnel and facilities
to meet Washington's demands on the embassy. In Washington, DOS
led the interagency coordination process, but President Bush appointed
Zalmay Khalilzad, an Afghan-born American on the NSC, as his per-

---

[28] Goodson (2006, p. 151); Vaishnav (2004, pp. 250–251). See also UNSC Resolution 1510,
on the situation in Afghanistan, October 13, 2003.

[29] Katzman (2006, p. 18).

sonal envoy. As a White House–based official, Khalilzad operated largely independently of DOS. Nor was DOS in any position to oversee DoD activities, something that could be done only from the White House, which was not so inclined.

In the course of 2002, President Bush had become increasingly concerned about the slow pace of Afghan reconstruction. The Pentagon and the Vice President's office blamed the lack of progress on mismanagement by DOS and USAID.[30] Those agencies, by contrast, blamed the Pentagon for its refusal to secure the countryside or even permit international peacekeepers to do so.

An April 2002 report by the Congressional Research Service found that

> [t]he Administration has not yet given a detailed indication of what role it envisions for the United States in the political, economic, and social reconstruction of Afghanistan beyond current plans for emergency food and agriculture assistance, assistance in the formation of a new national army, and anti-narcotics aid.[31]

With no clearly defined strategy, the civilian side of the implementation could not hope to challenge the military for attention or resources.

Despite the disparity in funding, the United States, with the support of a broad international humanitarian-assistance effort, did manage to avert the humanitarian catastrophe that was expected to accompany the war. October 4, 2001, Assistant Secretary of State Christina Rocca declared a "complex humanitarian disaster in Afghanistan," which prompted a multiagency assistance effort that included USAID's Office of Foreign Disaster Assistance, Food for Peace, and the Office of Transition Initiatives; the U.S. Department of Agriculture; the Centers for Disease Control and Prevention; and, within DOS, the Bureau

---

[30] Fukuyama (2006, pp. 8–9).

[31] Richard P. Cronin, *Afghanistan: Challenges and Options for Reconstructing a Stable and Moderate State*, CRS Report for Congress, Washington, D.C.: Congressional Research Service, April 24, 2002, p. 2.

of Population, Refugees, and Migration, the Office of Humanitarian Demining Programs, and the Bureau of International Narcotics and Law Enforcement Affairs. USAID's initial plan had five goals:

- to reduce death rates in Afghanistan
- to minimize population movements (of both internally displaced persons and refugees)
- to lower and then stabilize food prices so that food in markets would be more accessible
- to ensure that aid reached those for whom it was intended
- to increase the effectiveness of developmental relief projects, enabling them to move beyond emergency relief and focus on long-overdue reconstruction projects.

The effort was successful in averting humanitarian disaster in Afghanistan: "[R]efugee flows were handled effectively, food was delivered to the hungry, and the first steps were taken toward stabilizing a country that had endured decades of war."[32] In August 2002, USAID developed an interim strategy and action plan, but it had no measurable goals, time frames, resources, responsibilities, objective measures, or means to evaluate the progress of the wider mission in Afghanistan. The requirement for a full strategy and action plan was waived in February 2002, January 2003, and again in February 2004, undermining USAID's efforts in achieving long-term development goals and the provision of accountability for agency programs.[33]

By the end of 2002, Congress, like the President, had become frustrated with the slow pace of progress and the lack of a strategy for Afghanistan. In response, it passed the Afghanistan Freedom Support Act,[34] strongly urging the President to designate a coordinator within DOS who would be responsible for the following:

---

[32] Oliker et al. (2004, pp. 1, 57).

[33] U.S. General Accounting Office, *Afghanistan Reconstruction: Deteriorating Security and Limited Resources Have Impeded Progress; Improvements in U.S. Strategy Needed*, Washington, D.C., GAO-04-403, June 2004, pp. 34–35.

[34] Public Law 107-327, Afghanistan Freedom Support Act of 2002, December 4, 2002.

- designing an overall strategy to advance U.S. interests in Afghanistan
- ensuring program and policy coordination among U.S. agencies carrying out the policies set forth in the act
- pursuing Afghanistan-assistance coordination with other countries and international organizations
- ensuring proper management, implementation, and oversight by agencies responsible for Afghan assistance programs.[35]

In response to the Afghanistan Freedom Support Act, the President published a strategy for Afghanistan in February 2003. It was very broad, lacking any operational details or measurable goals. Nor was an official named with adequate authority to perform the coordination tasks outlined by Congress. In June 2003, after the United States collected "precise and comprehensive data" on the "ethnic, regional, and political makeup of the Kabul administration," DOS finally published its first "mission performance plan" for U.S. efforts in Afghanistan from 2003 to 2006. This was the first document to describe "specific tactics and activities to be undertaken" and assign "responsibility for each activity to USAID and other offices of the agencies housed in the U.S. Embassy in Afghanistan." It defined "baseline data, performance indicators, and targets for achieving each performance goal." The DOS plan was "an authoritative, integrated interagency country strategy document, prepared by the U.S. embassy country team."[36]

In late 2003, Khalilzad was sent to Kabul to replace Finn. He brought with him a sharply increased aid budget, which he was able to apply toward the plan's main objectives:

- working with the Karzai government to balance representation of personnel from all regions in the staffs of central ministries
- working with the Kabul government to remove and replace unqualified or disloyal governors and local chiefs of police

---

[35] U.S. General Accounting Office (2004, pp. 8–9).

[36] U.S. General Accounting Office (2004, p. 33); Starr (2006, p. 121).

- pressuring warlords to turn over tax receipts to the central government, promoting cantonment of heavy weapons under the UN disarmament program, and making deals with the Karzai government
- supporting the Afghan government's demand that NGO activity henceforth be fully coordinated with Afghan officials at both the national and local levels and that NGOs be held fully accountable to national laws and local officials
- retraining and upgrading local civil servants and police through extensive new programs at the national and local levels, enabling them to interact lawfully, honestly, and productively with the local populace, businesses, and voluntary groups and organizations.[37]

This shift in strategy was nothing short of fundamental. The Pentagon accepted that it had to participate in achieving these political goals in addition to continuing its efforts to hunt terrorists. The interagency team in Kabul had a plan that was jointly developed, that would be jointly executed, and that finally called for measures to strengthen instead of undermine the Afghan central government.

To help achieve these goals at the tactical level, in 2003, DoD created three provincial reconstruction teams (PRTs), each made up of 50–100 U.S. soldiers and civilian specialists in development, diplomacy, and economics. The purpose of the teams was to improve reconstruction efforts at the local level, allow the central government's influence to extend outside the capital, and better measure local and regional progress.

Although the PRTs had their shortcomings—100 soldiers could not adequately promote security for an entire region—their early achievements were encouraging, and other PRTs were stood up throughout the country.[38] Ultimately, the results were mixed, with PRTs located in highly insecure areas having little time for reconstruction efforts. But the prevailing opinion was that the "best PRTs make a contribution in creating ties with community groups and helping to settle or at

---

[37] Starr (2006, p. 120).

[38] Vaishnav (2004, p. 251).

least mitigate local disputes." Some humanitarian NGOs, concerned about the safety of their staffs, which they perceived as linked to their apparent impartiality, felt that the PRTs dangerously blurred the line between military and humanitarian objectives.[39] Overall, the creation of the PRTs was nevertheless seen as a success. In late 2003, Lieutenant General David Barno, the U.S. coalition commander, made the PRTs the backbone of his strategy, embracing in all but name the sort of peacekeeping mission that the administration had earlier disdained.[40] By 2006, 24 PRTs were operating in Afghanistan, with half staffed and run by allies and some run by civilians.[41]

During 2003, several Washington-based committees were created or reorganized in an attempt to improve the interagency implementation effort in Afghanistan. In October, a National Security Decision Directive eliminated the NSC policy coordination committee on Afghanistan and established the Afghanistan Interagency Operating Group, which met daily to coordinate efforts on a wide range of policy, programming, and funding issues among DoD, DOS, the Department of the Treasury, USAID, the NSC staff, the Office of Management and Budget, and other participating agencies. Personality problems that plagued the policy coordination committee were less an issue in the Afghanistan Interagency Operating Group, and thus the latter was more successful at working through interagency issues.

Also in October 2003, the Afghanistan Reconstruction Office was renamed the Office for Afghanistan and assumed responsibility for the functions outlined in the Afghanistan Freedom Support Act of 2002. That same month, a 15-person Afghanistan Reconstruction Group was established in the U.S. Embassy in Afghanistan to provide advisers to the Afghan government. This group, which included several senior experts with impressive private-sector experience, was meant to oversee a wide range of efforts, including advising the Afghan government on

---

[39] Marvin G. Weinbaum, "Rebuilding Afghanistan: Impediments, Lessons, and Prospects," in Francis Fukuyama, ed., *Nation-Building: Beyond Afghanistan and Iraq*, Baltimore, Md.: Johns Hopkins University Press, 2006, p. 130.

[40] Goodson (2006, p. 151).

[41] Katzman (2006, pp. 24, 46).

rebuilding the army and police, disarmament, demobilization, resettle-
ment, rule of law, elections, agriculture, demining, industry, health,
higher education, and major government infrastructure. Ultimately,
the advisers who were sent to the Afghanistan Reconstruction Group,
while experts in their fields, had little knowledge of Afghanistan and,
faced with deteriorating security, rarely left the confines of the capital.
Many advisers also faced bureaucratic restrictions, requiring authorization from Washington for projects costing more than $25,000. The
group was phased out by 2006.[42]

The colocation of the U.S. military command and the U.S.
embassy aided on-the-ground civil-military coordination. Lieutenant General Barno occupied an office next to Ambassador Khalilzad.
Cooperation at the top of the U.S. country team trickled down to
operational-level civilian and military officers and was enhanced by
the tactical-level interagency cooperation in the PRTs.[43] Barno's staff
provided planning expertise that informed the DOS mission performance plan, helping to ensure that it would be executable and that its
effects would be measurable.

Transition

A sovereign, if weak and dependent, Afghan government was put in
place even before the conclusion of the initial military campaign. The
subsequent UN-led effort to ground this new regime on popular sovereignty and free elections has been the single most unequivocally
successful element of the international community's engagement in
Afghanistan. Embracing traditional Afghan arrangements, an emergency *loya jirga* was held in June 2002. Across Afghanistan, 381 dis-
tricts selected 1,550 delegates who agreed to a unitary government and
presidential rule, confirming Karzai, until then only the chair of the
interim administration, as provisional president. In October 2002,
the 35-member constitutional commission drafted a permanent constitution. In UN-run caucuses throughout Afghanistan, 502 delegates

---

[42] Katzman (2006, p. 10); U.S. General Accounting Office (2004, pp. 31, 74); Weinbaum
(2006, pp. 137–138).

[43] Goodson (2006, p. 165).

were selected to attend a second, constitutional *loya jirga*. This group met from December 13, 2003, to January 4, 2004, and with only minor changes approved the constitution. On October 9, 2004, a presidential election was held, and, on November 3, Karzai was declared the winner. On September 18, 2005, parliamentary elections were held, with the results announced in November and the parliament convening for the first time on December 18, 2005, completing Afghanistan's journey from deposed Taliban regime to democratically elected government.[44]

Even as Afghanistan's political transition moved forward, however, the security situation was deteriorating. Year after year, the number of terrorist attacks increased, reaching a level three times higher in 2007 than in 2002. The rise in violence was particularly acute between 2005 and 2006. During this period, the number of suicide attacks quadrupled, from 27 to 139; remotely detonated bombings more than doubled, from 783 to 1,677; and armed attacks nearly tripled, from 1,558 to 4,542. Just as the United States and its allies were agreeing to extend ISAF beyond Kabul, the nature of that force's mission began to shift from peacekeeping to counterinsurgency.

The resumption of civil war in Afghanistan can be attributed to two fundamental causes. One was the failure of the government of Pakistan to prevent the Taliban and al Qaeda from reorganizing, recruiting, financing, training, and operating out of sanctuaries on its territory. The other was the failure of the United States, the Karzai administration, and the rest of the international community to take advantage of the lull in violence following the 2001 collapse of the Taliban to project government services, including security, into the countryside. As a result, when insurgent groups eventually resumed operations in the south and east of the country, they encountered little in the way of government infrastructure or popular commitment to a regime in Kabul, which had done little to protect their safety or prosperity.

---

[44] Katzman (2006, pp. 8–9).

Iraq

Planning for the Postwar Period

On November 21, 2001, less than a week after the fall of Kabul, President Bush directed Secretary of Defense Rumsfeld to update the Iraq war plan. One week later, Rumsfeld told General Tommy Franks, the USCENTCOM commander, to develop such a plan. Over the next 16 months, General Franks's staff produced a series of evolving drafts culminating in OPLAN Cobra II, which obtained presidential approval in January 2003.[45]

USCENTCOM envisaged, following the fall of Baghdad and end of major combat operations, an initial two- to three-month "stabilization" phase, followed by an 18- to 24-month "recovery" phase, during which most U.S. forces would be withdrawn. The intention of these phase IV operations was to make maximum use of Iraqi resources, including the army and police. Indigenous security forces would gradually take over from the United States.[46]

Initially, General Franks told his commanders that DOS would take the lead in deciding how to rebuild Iraq's political institutions and infrastructure. In the summer of 2002, the JCS informed Franks that he would be in charge of planning for the postwar period.[47] During the fall of 2002, Franks had his ground commander, Lieutenant General David McKiernan, develop a more extended plan for phase IV. McKiernan's staff began a series of war games to test the plan's assumptions and identify potential shortcomings that could be rectified prior to the initiation of hostilities. By the middle of February 2003, his staff concluded that "the campaign would produce conditions at odds with

---

[45] These plans were titled "Generated Start," "Running Start," and "Hybrid." On the history of this planning process, see Gordon and Trainor (2006, pp. 24–54, 75–117) and Franks (2004, pp. 382–415).

[46] Gordon and Trainor (2006, p. 68).

[47] It is unclear precisely when USCENTCOM was given this order. Thomas Ricks, quoting then–deputy chief of planning Colonel John Agoglia, puts the date of the Joint Staff directive at July 2002. Gordon and Trainor (2006), however, place these instructions in August. See Thomas E. Ricks, *Fiasco: The American Military Adventure in Iraq*, New York: Penguin, 2006, p. 78, and Gordon and Trainor (2006, p. 139).

meeting the strategic objectives" established by USCENTCOM. In particular, the "joint campaign was specifically designed to break all control mechanisms of the regime," which called into question the ability to rely on Iraqi institutions in the early part of phase IV.[48] Although this assessment did not foresee all challenges that would confront U.S. forces during the transition from phase III to phase IV, it identified a number of actions to be addressed in the OPLAN, including "planning to control the borders, analyzing what key areas and infrastructure should be immediately protected, and allocating adequate resources to quickly re-establish post-war control throughout Iraq." However, McKiernan's staff failed to persuade him to seek a fundamental reshaping of the fast-approaching combat operations to address such potential contingencies.[49]

McKiernan did develop OPLAN Eclipse II as a sequel to the existing Cobra II plan against the possibility that the optimistic end-state conditions envisioned under Cobra II would not materialize. Under Eclipse II, during the first 60 days of fighting, coalition forces would "secure key infrastructure," "support the maintenance of public order and safety," "support the restoration of critical utilities/basic services," "'empower' selected Iraqi officials," and "begin reintegration of the Iraqi military." An Iraqi consultative council would be established to help govern Iraq until an independent Iraqi government was established.[50] While more realistic than its predecessor, particularly with regard to its appraisal of the potential security challenges that coalition forces would face in the postwar period, Eclipse II continued to rely heavily on the Iraqi military and police to maintain public order and assumed that Iraqi civil authorities would continue to run local

---

[48] LTC Steven W. Peterson, "Central but Inadequate: The Application of Theory in Operation Iraqi Freedom," thesis, National Defense University, 2004, p. 10.

[49] Peterson (2004, pp. 10, 11). As Peterson notes, "The war was not yet started, let alone finished, when these issues were being raised. Only a fool would propose hurting the war fighting effort to address post-war conditions that might or might not occur" (p. 11); Also quoted in Gordon and Trainor (2006, p. 146).

[50] Gordon and Trainor (2006, p. 145), quoting a February 28, 2003, briefing on Coalition Forces Land Component Command stability operations.

and regional essential services. Moreover, this plan was still not completed when Baghdad fell on April 9, 2003.

Whereas USCENTCOM did not begin postwar planning until the fall of 2002, civilian agencies had been conducting their own studies since the spring.[51] In March 2002, DOS announced the formation of the Future of Iraq Project, which brought together groups of Iraqi expatriates and civilian experts in meetings starting in July 2002. In May 2002, the CIA began a series of games designed to look at possible scenarios for a post–Saddam Hussein Iraq. By mid-September, USAID had several teams working on postwar planning with relief organizations and NGOs that were participating in weekly coordination meetings.

In August 2002, Condoleezza Rice took control of an interagency group that had been formed by General George Casey, then the head of the Policy Directorate (J5) on the Joint Staff. Renamed the Executive Steering Group (ESG) and chaired by Frank Miller, the NSC's senior director for defense policy and arms control, this interdepartmental committee included officials from the NSC staff, DOS, DoD, JCS, the CIA, and the Office of the Vice President. The deputy under secretary–level ESG met three times a week and addressed a wide range of political-military planning issues, such as securing basing, access, and overflight rights; accelerating military construction; identifying allied capabilities that could contribute to military operations; and postwar planning.

In addition, the NSC staff formed several other interagency groups, including the Iraq Political-Military Cell (IPMC) and the Humanitarian/Reconstruction Group (HRG). The IPMC sat below the ESG and brought together working-level officials from each of the agencies participating in the ESG. The IPMC was never intended to do any independent planning, but rather to enable agencies throughout the U.S. government to conduct their own planning efforts within a coherent strategic framework. The HRG was cochaired by Elliott Abrams of the NSC and Robin Cleveland of the Office of Management and Budget and included ESG representatives from the Treasury Department, the

---

[51] Fukuyama (2006, p. 9).

Department of Justice, and USAID. The HRG focused on providing humanitarian relief in the immediate postwar period and reconstruction assistance over the longer term.[52]

Although the various working groups represented a fairly significant effort to reach interagency consensus on strategic guidance for Iraq, none of these committees was able to fully coordinate efforts across the civil-military divide. ESG meetings were not always attended by every agency nor by the same representatives from one meeting to the next. The IPMC spent much of its time on postwar issues, using the work of the HRG as a basis for its efforts, but these matters rarely made it to the ESG. The ESG focused primarily on war planning and devoted little attention to the postcombat phase.[53] Consequently, most of the postwar planning at lower levels was not discussed or approved by senior interagency representatives and thus was often not translated into action.

In late 2002, President Bush made the controversial decision to place the Pentagon in charge of all civil and military planning for postwar Iraq. Secretary Rumsfeld had proposed that U.S. efforts in postwar Iraq should be run solely by DoD, a proposal that was endorsed by the NSC/PC in October 2002. It was agreed that Deputy National Security Advisor Stephen Hadley would draft a directive for the President to sign, formalizing Rumsfeld's move.

At the time, neither Secretary of State Powell nor his deputy, Richard Armitage, objected. Despite the concerns of those within the DOS bureaucracy, Powell and Armitage felt that the Pentagon had the money and resources to devote to the postwar mission and therefore was entitled to run it.[54] Thus, for the first time since the end of the

---

[52] On the formation and roles of these interagency working groups, see Near East South Asia Center for Strategic Studies, National Defense University, "Pre-War Planning for Post-War Iraq," undated; Gordon and Trainor (2006, pp. 148–149); and Ricks (2006, pp. 48–49).

[53] Gordon and Trainor (2006, pp. 148–149).

[54] Gordon and Trainor (2006, p. 149). Gordon and Trainor imply that Powell may have relinquished control of postwar Iraq to leave the burden of the war's messy aftermath to his bureaucratic counterpart.

German and Japanese occupations, DOS would not oversee the civil aspects of postwar reconstruction.

The President's decision in this matter was probably influenced by his frustration over the slow pace of progress in Afghanistan in the summer of 2002 and the perception that this was caused by dual lines of authority for military and civilian officials that inhibited effective coordination.[55] He may also have been concerned that DOS was unenthusiastic about the coming war and might drag its feet if charged with any essential aspect of preparations for it.

Another controversy regarding the interagency planning process revolved around the DOS Future of Iraq Project. Led by Thomas S. Warrick, a special adviser to the department's Office of Northern Gulf Affairs, the project was announced in March 2002. Meetings were held from July 2002 until April 2003 and involved more than 200 expatriate Iraqi experts working in 17 groups on topics as diverse as public health, humanitarian requirements immediately following the fall of Saddam's regime, oil and energy, defense policy, education, media, agriculture, and democratic development. Project members met 33 times in Washington, D.C., and London and produced arguably the single most comprehensive assessment of postwar requirements conducted by the U.S. government.

In the end, the project's 13 volumes ran to 2,500 pages, allowing journalists and critics of the Bush administration to select a number of assessments that appear prescient in hindsight. For example, reporter James Fallows argued, "More than a year earlier, long before combat began, the explicit recommendations and implicit lessons of the Future of Iraq project had given the U.S. government a very good idea of what political conflicts it could expect in Iraq."[56]

---

[55] Nora Bensahel, "Mission Not Accomplished: What Went Wrong with Iraqi Reconstruction," *Journal of Strategic Studies*, Vol. 29, No. 3, June 2006, pp. 458–459; and Fukuyama (2006, p. 10).

[56] James Fallows, "Blind into Baghdad," *Atlantic Monthly*, January–February 2004. Although, given that the first meeting of the Future of Iraq project did not take place until nine months before the initiation of combat operations, Fallows is guilty of some inaccuracy. See also Eric Schmitt and Joel Brinkley, "State Dept. Study Foresaw Trouble Now Plaguing

Most analysts familiar with the contents of the study dismissed the notion that the project's recommendations constituted an executable plan. Robert Perito, a former DOS official and leading expert on postconflict police work, said, "It was a good idea. It brought the exiles together, a lot of smart people, and its reports were very impressive. But the project never got to the point where things were in place that could be implemented."[57] David Kay read the study and summarized it, saying, "It was unimplementable. It was a series of essays to describe what the future could be. It was not a plan to hand to a task force and say 'go implement.' If it had been carried out it would not have made a difference." Colonel Paul Hughes, who would become Lieutenant General Jay Garner's chief planner, agreed: "While it produced some useful background information it had no chance of really influencing the post-Saddam phase of the war."[58] Upon arriving in Baghdad, Ambassador Ryan Crocker, who was the Deputy Assistant Secretary of State for Near Eastern Affairs and deeply involved with the study, told Ambassador Paul Bremer that the Future of Iraq Project "was never intended as a postwar plan."[59]

If the Future of Iraq project was not itself a fully realized plan for the reconstruction of Iraq, it certainly contained elements from which such a plan might have been assembled. No effort was made to do so. The project's findings were not entirely ignored by the rest of the U.S. government, however. The issues highlighted by the project's working groups were discussed in the NSC-sponsored IWGs. Pentagon policy was formulated in conjunction with the recommendations of the NSC's Democratic Principles Working Group. And the study was eventually conveyed to the U.S. officials who administered Iraq.[60]

Iraq," *New York Times*, October 19, 2003, and David Phillips, *Losing Iraq*, Boulder, Colo.: Westview Press, 2005.

[57] In David Rieff, "Blueprint for a Mess," *New York Times Magazine*, November 2, 2003.

[58] In Gordon and Trainor (2006, p. 159).

[59] L. Paul Bremer III, with Malcolm McConnell, *My Year in Iraq: The Struggle to Build a Future of Hope*, New York: Simon and Schuster, 2006a, p. 25.

[60] Michael Rubin, "Iraq in Books: Review Essay," *Middle East Quarterly*, Vol. 14, No. 2, Spring 2007, p. 25; Gordon and Trainor (2006, p. 159).

What did not occur was the integration of civilian and military planning across agency lines into a single strategy for the postwar period.

Within DoD, Rumsfeld assigned the job of postwar planning to Douglas Feith, his Under Secretary of Defense for Policy. Feith was given the goal of bringing about "unity of effort and unity of leadership for the full range of reconstruction activities that need to be performed in order to say that the mission is over and the troops can leave."[61] In August 2002, Feith expanded the Office of Northern Gulf Affairs in DoD's Office of Near East and South Asia from four to 14 people to handle the increased workload of planning Operation Iraqi Freedom. The expanded office was renamed the Office of Special Plans (OSP) in order not to draw attention to the fact that the Pentagon was considering the possibility of war and its aftermath in Iraq while simultaneously seeking international support from the UN.[62] Through the end of 2002, the OSP produced guidance on issues ranging from debaathification to the future of the Iraqi army but little that could be considered an executable plan. In language echoing Roosevelt's admonitions to Cordell Hull regarding planning for the occupation of Germany, Feith defended the lack of specificity in OSP's planning by citing Secretary Rumsfeld's strategic theme of uncertainty as the reason that workable plans were not developed:

> You will not find a single piece of paper . . . that says, "Mr. Secretary or Mr. President, let us tell you what postwar Iraq is going to look like, and here is what we need plans for." If you tried that, you would get thrown out of Rumsfeld's office so fast—if you ever went in there and said, "Let me tell you what something's

---

[61] Bob Woodward, *State of Denial*, New York: Simon and Schuster, 2006, p. 91.

[62] Feith later explained, "The Special Plans Office was called Special Plans because, at the time, calling it the Iraqi Planning Office might have undercut our diplomatic efforts" (in Mark Fineman, Robin Wright, and Doyle McManus, "Preparing for War, Stumbling to Peace," *Los Angeles Times*, July 18, 2003). The OSP later became a source of controversy when several journalists falsely identified it as an intelligence collection unit. See Seymour Hersh, "Selective Intelligence," *New Yorker*, May 12, 2003, and Rieff (2003).

going to look like in the future," you wouldn't get to your next sentence![63]

Feith himself was known more as an articulate advocate and tenacious bureaucrat than as an administrator. His staff, in any case, had no experience and very little of the capacity needed to organize and run a massive operation of this sort.[64]

Once charged with overall responsibility for both civil and military planning, DoD blocked several efforts to plan across agency lines. Rumsfeld rejected a number of DOS nominees to serve under Garner in the Office of Reconstruction and Humanitarian Assistance (ORHA). He specifically told Garner that he could not attach Warwick, organizer of the Future of Iraq Project, to his staff. When Garner insisted, Rumsfeld said that he was acting under instructions from a "higher authority."

Despite agreement in October 2002 among NSC principals to accord DoD responsibility for postwar planning, it was not until late January 2003 that President Bush formally assigned the Pentagon this authority. NSPD 24 established ORHA, the first organization specifically dedicated to postwar planning for Iraq.[65] Retired Army Lieutenant General Jay Garner was selected to head ORHA and directed by NSPD 24 to provide "detailed planning across the spectrum of issues that the United States Government would face with respect to the postwar administration of Iraq."[66] Garner had commanded U.S. military humanitarian operations in Northern Iraq a decade earlier and was thus familiar with at least that part of the country.

Feith told Garner that a wide range of planning efforts had already been conducted throughout the U.S. government and that his

---

[63] In Fallows (2004). Roosevelt told his Secretary of State, "I dislike making detailed plans for a country we do not yet occupy" (in Beschloss, 2002, p. 159).

[64] Fukuyama (2006, p. 10). On the managerial problems within the Office of the Under Secretary of Defense for Policy, see Rowan Scarborough, "Pentagon Policy-Makers Battle Waning Morale," *Washington Times*, August 12, 2002, and Ricks (2006, pp. 76–78).

[65] George W. Bush, National Security Presidential Directive 24, on postwar Iraq reconstruction, Washington, D.C.: White House, January 20, 2003.

[66] G. W. Bush (2003).

job would be to coordinate and integrate these previous efforts rather than generating new plans.[67] After agreeing to take the job, Garner started assembling his staff, initially comprised largely of other retired military and civilian personnel. Filling out the organization proved to be an ongoing challenge. Although NSPD 24 ordered 10 federal agencies to provide experts to ORHA, directing that they should be senior enough to oversee coordination throughout their own agencies, most departments took their time in selecting these representatives. As the ORHA staff started assembling, they encountered administrative difficulties in finding space, furniture, computers, and communication facilities; assigning responsibilities; establishing hierarchies; and ensuring that everyone was getting paid, had travel orders, and was prepared to move on short notice. These challenges left little time for substantive issues and long-term planning.

Once ORHA was up and running, Garner identified several issues that it would have to be prepared to address in the immediate aftermath of the war. First and foremost, he expressed concern that the war would trigger a major refugee crisis, especially if Saddam Hussein used chemical weapons. Garner also worried that Saddam might set fire to Iraq's oil fields and destroy dams throughout the country, that epidemics of cholera and other diseases would erupt as sanitation and electrical systems failed, and that starvation would spread as the food-distribution system broke down.[68] In these humanitarian concerns, ORHA was able to draw on the extensive preexisting interagency planning efforts.

Garner also identified one other major problem: ORHA would have to ensure that the Iraqi ministries continued to function between the fall of Saddam's regime and the establishment of a new government.[69] Saddam's regime depended on a highly centralized bureaucracy in which all important decisions were made in Baghdad. It was assumed that the seniormost levels of ministry leadership—the minister and some senior Ba'athist officials—could be removed and replaced

---

[67] Fineman, Wright, and McManus (2003).

[68] Lieutenant General Jay Garner, *Frontline*, interview transcript, July 17, 2003.

[69] Garner (2003).

without substantially undermining the work of the ministries. The large civil-service staffs in the ministries would keep running under new leadership. As Condoleezza Rice noted, "The concept was that we would defeat the army, but the institutions would hold, everything from ministries to police forces."[70] A ministerial advisory team, consisting of a senior adviser from a coalition government, expatriate Iraqi technocrats, and the most senior Iraqi technocrat remaining in the ministry after the top-level Ba'athists were removed, would be established for each ministry.

ORHA divided planning into three areas: humanitarian assistance, reconstruction, and civil administration. Because of the dire predictions of humanitarian disasters, such as food shortages, disease, massive numbers of refugees and internally displaced persons, consequence management following the use of chemical or biological agents, and widespread oil-well fires, Garner focused most of his effort in preparing the humanitarian-assistance mission.[71]

On February 21–22, 2003, ORHA convened an interagency rehearsal for the postwar period at the National Defense University in Washington, D.C. More than 200 participants from agencies across the government participated in the two-day conference. The meeting was intended as an opportunity for each agency to pitch its ideas about how to proceed, and, consequently, there was little synchronization of plans. Garner's deputy, retired General Ron Adams, recorded in his notes following the gathering, "Faulty assumptions. Overly optimistic. Lack of reality."[72] Garner himself later noted that the meeting exposed "tons of problems" with planning and coordination efforts.[73]

One particularly serious shortcoming was identified. It was proving very difficult to get various organizations within the U.S. govern-

---

[70] In Michael R. Gordon, "The Strategy to Secure Iraq Did Not Foresee a 2nd War," *New York Times*, October 19, 2004.

[71] George Packer, *The Assassins' Gate: America in Iraq*, New York: Farrar, Straus and Giroux, 2005, p. 122. See also Lieutenant General Jay Garner, *Frontline*, interview transcript, August 11, 2006.

[72] Woodward (2006, p. 126).

[73] Fineman, Wright, and McManus (2003).

ment to provide personnel for the ministerial teams, especially given the tight time constraints but also because of bureaucratic resistance by various agencies to placing their personnel under DoD control, something they had never done before.[74] In this regard, the meeting highlighted the fact that the issue of who would provide security for civilian officials in the postwar period, typically a DOS responsibility, remained unresolved. British Major General Albert Whitley, McKiernan's deputy for postwar issues, warned that the coalition would probably suffer three to five casualties per week after the fall of Baghdad and that some of these would be civilians, which led some DOS aides to say that they could not participate under those circumstances.

Dick Mayer, representing the Justice Department, proposed a plan calling for some 5,000 international police advisers to be rushed to Iraq to fill the law-enforcement vacuum after the collapse of the Iraqi government. Based on the Clinton administration's experiences in Haiti, Bosnia, and Kosovo, this number was actually rather low. However, when Garner took this plan to the White House, it was decided that only 1,500 unarmed advisers would be sent to train the Iraqi police force instead. This number was eventually pared down even further to a 50-expert fact-finding mission.[75]

Garner, similar to DoD, planned to keep the Iraqi army in place to assist with reconstruction projects and avoid unleashing a flood of unemployed young men into the general population. In the area of civil administration, Garner planned to remove the top two Ba'athists in each ministry. Garner intended to assume responsibility in Baghdad in April; appoint an interim Iraqi government; select an Iraqi constitutional convention; have the Iraqis write a new democratic constitution, ratify it, and hold nationwide democratic elections; and hand over sovereignty to the democratically elected Iraqi government no later than August 2003. This schedule was based on three assumptions: first, that

---

[74] Conversely, procedures for assigning other agencies' personnel to DOS missions, defining who pays for what, and establishing exactly what degree of subordination is involved have long been in place. No such arrangements existed for assigning other agencies' personnel to a DoD-run nonmilitary operation.

[75] Gordon and Trainor (2006, pp. 154, 157).

large numbers of Iraqi security forces would remain in place and support the occupation; second, that the rest of the international community would quickly deploy resources to Iraq and take over responsibilities from the U.S. military; and third, that an Iraqi government would form quickly, allowing the United States to hand off responsibility for governing the country shortly after the regime change. All these assumptions proved to be wrong.[76]

On March 10, President Bush and his advisers met to review the plans for postwar Iraq. Frank Miller, chair of the ESG, led the briefing. First, he explained, the United States wanted a firm program of debaathification. There were an estimated 1.5 million members of the party; however, only about 25,000, or the top 1 to 2 percent, were active members. These would be barred from government employment in the new Iraq. A truth and reconciliation commission would be established to shine light on the many atrocities that had occurred. Additionally, the United States could prosecute anyone for war crimes committed against U.S. personnel dating back to Desert Storm, and Iraqi courts could try war criminals for crimes against Iraqis or Kuwaitis. Finally, because the CIA had assessed the Iraqi police as professional and not aligned with Saddam Hussein, no U.S. personnel would be deployed to exercise police, judicial, or penal functions.

Two days later, Miller briefed the President on the plan for reshaping the Iraqi military. Three to five divisions would form the new Iraqi army, and they would initially be used as a national reconstruction force. The new Iraqi government would fund the rebuilding of the Iraqi military, and, if necessary, allies would be asked to contribute. Iraqi intelligence services would be consolidated into a single agency, a new defense ministry, which would be led by a civilian. The police would work for the interior ministry. Finally, there would be no transfer to UN control or international administration in Iraq. Control would pass quickly from the United States back to Iraqi leaders. There was no plan B, nor any discussion of what would happen if the underlying assumptions turned out to be false.[77]

---

[76] Ricks (2006, pp. 104–105, 110).

[77] Gordon and Trainor (2006, pp. 161–163).

Allies

Other than the UK, no ally contributed forces sufficient to give its government much influence over U.S. policy. Even the British role was more limited than its nominal status as one of two legally coequal occupying powers might suggest. Almost three-dozen governments contributed forces to the Multi-National Force–Iraq, but their total personnel peaked at just over 25,000, including the sizable British contingent. Twenty nations besides the United States have suffered fatalities from enemy action during Operation Iraqi Freedom. However, most foreign troops operated under extremely restrictive rules of engagement, patrolling the more secure areas of the country.

Neither did Washington seek to consult neighboring governments about its plans for the future of Iraq, as it had done successfully at the Bonn conference on Afghanistan. The administration was already talking about making Iraq a democratic model for the Middle East, the effect of which could ultimately be similar changes among most of its neighbors. Therefore, this was not a project that was likely to appeal to neighboring regimes.

The UN also played a less significant role in Iraq than in Afghanistan, in part due to the controversy associated with the invasion and in part due to the administration's greater desire to shape the postwar environment there.[78]

On March 3, 2003, Garner visited UN headquarters in New York, without the White House's or Pentagon's knowledge, to see what support he could expect during the postwar period. UN Deputy Secretary-General Louise Fréchette told him that the UN was not seeking any role outside of providing immediate humanitarian relief. Garner asked whether ORHA could get a UN liaison officer. The answer was no. The UN, which had been central to ushering a new government into Afghanistan, did not want to get involved in regime change in Iraq in the absence of a UNSC mandate, which the United States and

---

[78] The administration's resistance to a substantial UN role in Iraq was gradually overcome, and, by mid-2004, it would seek a more prominent role for the organization. The UN itself also labored under some disadvantages in Iraq due to its role in imposing and administering sanctions in the previous decade.

the UK had not succeeded in securing.[79] The Bush administration nevertheless believed that military success in Iraq would attract the participation of the international community in the postwar effort.

On May 22, 2003, UNSC Resolution 1483 acknowledged the United States and Britain as occupying powers in Iraq and lifted UN sanctions against that country.[80] Sergio Vieira de Mello, chief of the UN mission, arrived in Iraq on June 3. Tragically, he was killed by a truck bomb on August 19, and the UN quickly reduced its presence in the country from 800 to 15 personnel. Other organizations, such as the World Bank, the International Monetary Fund, Oxfam, and Save the Children, also withdrew their personnel, citing the lack of security. On September 30, UN Secretary-General Kofi Annan told Washington that the transfer of sovereignty to an Iraqi interim government would be required before the UN would return in any numbers to Iraq.

By November, however, Washington was eager for the reestablishment of a high-level UN mission in Iraq. In late March, the UN dispatched Carina Perelli, the director of its Electoral Assistance Division. Lakhdar Brahimi arrived a week later to begin a marathon set of consultations involving Bremer, Ambassador Robert Blackwill, the Iraqi Governing Council (IGC), and other notable Iraqis. Brahimi was instrumental in the establishment of the Iraqi interim government, choosing virtually every cabinet minister himself, while Perelli selected the composition of the Independent Election Commission of Iraq, which oversaw Iraq's elections in January and December 2005.

Implementation

The lack of an integrated civil-military and interagency plan for the postwar phase left the military on the ground in Iraq with primary responsibility for many missions for which it was not well prepared. The 3rd Infantry Division's after-action report describes the situation it experienced upon arriving in Baghdad in April 2003:

---

[79] Woodward (2006, pp. 135–136).

[80] Bremer (2006a, p. 78). See also UNSC Resolution 1483, on the situation between Iraq and Kuwait, May 22, 2003.

> There was no guidance for restoring order in Baghdad, creating
> an interim government, hiring government and essential services
> employees, and ensuring that the judicial system was operational.
> The result was a power/authority vacuum created by our failure to
> immediately replace key government institutions. . . . The Presi-
> dent announced that our national goal was "regime change." Yet
> there was no timely plan prepared for the obvious consequences
> of a regime change.[81]

There were some early examples of success in the immediate postwar period. In Ar Rutbah, the local U.S. military leadership focused
on the people, empowered the local citizens, co-opted the existing
power structure in the town, emphasized humility and restraint, used
debaathification as a means for political change instead of a purge, and
enforced a strict rule that only U.S. military personnel were allowed
to carry weapons.[82] These isolated successes were the product of local
initiative and not a theaterwide coordinated plan, and when these military units were redeployed to other areas in Iraq or out of theater, the
implementation methods changed and the gains were short lived.

There were postwar plans in place to deal with the short-term
emergencies expected during the course of the war's prosecution.
ORHA was prepared for large numbers of internally displaced persons,
oil-well fires, and food shortages. Because the war had progressed so
quickly, however, none of the postwar disasters for which Garner and
his group had planned occurred.[83]

Before Garner even reached Iraq, efforts were already under way
in Washington to find a replacement for him. Rumsfeld was looking for a presidential envoy to Iraq who would operate as a "super-
administrator or even a viceroy."[84] On April 24, 2003, Rumsfeld called

---

[81] Ricks (2006, pp. 150–151).

[82] Ricks (2006, pp. 152–153).

[83] Bremer (2006a, p. 26).

[84] Woodward (2006, p. 166). However, Garner himself acknowledges that DoD had been
upfront with him at the start that this would be the case. According to Garner, General
Ronald Yaggi of the Office of the Secretary of Defense told him in the first call that he
received about the ORHA job, "'I need to tell you up front that you probably will never

Garner to tell him that he was being superseded by L. Paul Bremer, who would be the President's envoy to Iraq. This was not a complete surprise to Garner, who had always known that he would be succeeded by a more senior figure, but it occurred more quickly and with less notice than he expected. On May 9, 2003, Bremer was officially designated as the President's envoy, reporting through the Secretary of Defense and "empowered with 'all executive, legislative, and judicial functions' in Iraq."[85]

While Bremer was in Washington preparing to go Iraq, he met with Douglas Feith, who shared with him a draft debaathification order intended for Garner to issue. Bremer asked Feith to wait and let him issue it once he got to Iraq. Bremer recalled that Rumsfeld said that it was to be carried out "even if implementing it causes administrative inconvenience." On May 16, Bremer issued Coalition Provisional Authority (CPA) Order Number 1, De-Ba'athification of Iraqi Society.[86] This decree excluded the top four levels of the party membership, which the CPA estimated to be approximately 1 percent of all party members, or 20,000 people, from public employment.

The debaathification order also stated that the top three layers of management in every national government ministry, affiliated corporation, and government institution would be reviewed for possible connections to the Ba'ath party. Any of these managers found to be "full members" of the party would be removed from their government positions, though they would be free to work elsewhere. The order provided that Bremer or any of his designees could grant exceptions on a case-by-case basis.[87]

---

deploy to Iraq,' because at that point, [it was looking like it would be] somebody with name recognition, probably a former governor" (Garner, 2006).

[85] Bremer (2006a, pp. 12–13).

[86] Coalition Provisional Authority Order Number 1, De-Ba'athification of Iraqi Society, May 16, 2003.

[87] Bremer (2006a, pp. 40–41). Jay Garner and the former CIA Baghdad station chief put the number of banned Ba'athists closer to 50,000 and thought the order too severe (see Garner, 2006).

On May 23, Bremer signed CPA Order Number 2, Dissolution of Entities.[88] This directive dissolved all Iraqi national security ministries and military formations. Although the prewar plan had been to co-opt and reform the Iraqi army, once again, circumstances on the ground proved different from those planned. Whereas Iraqi army units were expected to capitulate on a large scale, in fact, none did so: Only 7,000 Iraqi soldiers were taken prisoner in Operation Iraqi Freedom, and the only Iraqi generals to formally surrender had no troops remaining on duty.[89] Because the Iraqi conscripts had returned home with their equipment and the postliberation looting had destroyed all Iraqi barracks, CPA officials believed that they would be creating a new refugee problem rather than a new army if they attempted to recall the demobilized soldiers. Moreover, they believed that, while the primarily Sunni officer corps might return to duty, the enlisted personnel, mostly conscripts and largely Shia, would not. Therefore, such a recall could seriously alienate the Shias and Kurds, who represented 80 percent of Iraq's population and had been the targets of army brutality in the past. Although Bremer sought the Pentagon's approval for this decision, the rest of the NSC members did not hear of it until it was announced. Thus, one of CPA's most critical decisions was made without review in any formal interagency process.[90]

Both at the White House and in the Pentagon, the initial feeling was that it would be better if Washington did not micromanage the CPA's efforts. NSC staffers were told that the interagency process would be carried out in Baghdad under Bremer, not in Washington. Zalmay Khalilzad, who had been working alongside Garner as a Presi-

---

[88] Coalition Provisional Authority Order Number 2, Dissolution of Entities, May 23, 2003.

[89] See Walter B. Slocombe, "To Build an Army," *Washington Post*, November 5, 2003, and Gordon and Trainor (2006, p. 462).

[90] Woodward (2006, pp. 194–195, 197–198). On the CPA decision to formally disband the Iraqi Army, see Bremer (2006a, pp. 54–59); Slocombe (2003); Dan Senor and Walter Slocombe, "Too Few Good Men," *New York Times*, November 17, 2005; and L. Paul Bremer III, "How I Didn't Dismantle Iraq's Army," *New York Times*, September 6, 2007. According to Bremer, however, Rumsfeld claims to have forwarded the paper that formed the basis for CPA Orders No. 1 and 2 to the National Security Advisor and Secretary of State.

dential envoy, stayed in Washington and ceased to work in that capacity. The ESG was disbanded, and the interagency group in Washington was no longer being consulted.

After CPA orders 1 and 2, Bremer's third major decision was to postpone the creation of a sovereign Iraqi government. Garner had appointed a seven-member leadership council comprised of four Shias, two Kurds, and one Sunni Arab in May 2003.[91] He and Khalilzad had made statements suggesting that the formation of an Iraqi government might occur in the near future. In mid-June, Bremer cancelled U.S. military plans for local elections in Najaf and later cancelled all local elections throughout Iraq, preferring to move at a more deliberate and orderly pace to anchor the local governments that would emerge from these ballots in some broader national scheme for democratization and the return of sovereignty. On July 13, Bremer established an Iraqi interim governing council comprised of 25 Iraqis, including 13 Shias, five Kurds, five Sunni Arabs, one Assyrian Christian, and one Turkman. The governing council was unable to agree on a single leader, and consequently, the presidency of the council rotated among nine council members on a monthly basis. The council also proved unable to exercise even the limited duties that Bremer assigned to it, including drafting a constitution.

As the CPA expanded its responsibilities, it quickly ran into significant staffing shortages. DoD proved unable to staff the operation with qualified personnel, and other agencies made only limited contributions. Many personnel who did arrive stayed for only brief periods, often no more than 90 days. This turnover greatly limited its effectiveness and ability to establish relationships with local Iraqis. Because the CPA was a unique, ad hoc organization, built by an agency that had no experience creating or running such an institution, much of its early effort was expended on issues of internal management.[92]

---

[91] Larry Diamond, *Squandered Victory: The American Occupation and the Bungled Effort to Bring Democracy to Iraq*, New York: Times Books, 2005, pp. 40–41. This was largely a codification of the preexisting leadership selected by the leading Iraqi exile and Kurdish parties, with the addition of Da'wa's leader, Ibrahim al-Ja'afari, who had refused to participate in previous opposition conferences.

[92] Fukuyama (2006, pp. 13).

Bremer wrote in his 2006 memoir that, "within weeks of arriving in Iraq, it was obvious that we needed a comprehensive plan of action, especially since Washington's prewar plans had been overtaken." Through June and early July, Bremer's planning staff developed a strategic plan with "clear mission objectives, metrics, and timetables" called "A Vision to Empower Iraqis." Bremer forwarded it to Rumsfeld on July 4, 2003. The CPA's end state was a "durable peace for a unified and stable, democratic Iraq, with a vibrant economy and a representative government which underpinned and protected freedoms." Security was the number-one priority, with the means to achieve security being the training of a police force and new Iraqi Army. Bremer also wanted to show every Iraqi how the U.S.-administered CPA had improved their daily lives and focused on the restoration of essential services, including power generation, schools, and hospitals. On July 22 and 23, Bremer briefed his strategic plan to the NSC/DC, and a copy of the plan was provided to every member of Congress.[93]

The CPA and Combined Joint Task Force 7 (CJTF 7)—the U.S. military command in Iraq—were never able to establish an entirely satisfactory working relationship, though personal relations between Bremer and Lieutenant General Rick Sanchez, the CJTF 7 commander, remained cordial. The U.S. presence in Iraq was a "jerry-rigged command structure, in which there was no one American official, civilian or military, on the ground in Iraq in charge of the overall American effort."[94] Since Sanchez and Bremer both reported to Secretary Rumsfeld, the unity of command that the Bush administration sought still lay in Washington rather than in Baghdad; its locus simply shifted from the White House to the Pentagon. The CPA's strategic plan was not initially coordinated with CJTF 7's strategic plan. It was not until September that the military attempted to align its plan with the CPA's. As late as May 2004, the Center for Army Lessons Learned reported, "[T]he common perception throughout the theater is that a roadmap for the rebuilding of Iraq does not exist. . . . If such a notional plan exists with the CPA, it has not been communicated adequately to

---

[93] Bremer (2006a, pp. 114–117).

[94] Ricks (2006, p. 174).

Coalition forces."[95] By mid-November, the CPA's strategic plan had grown from 57 pages to 153.[96]

During a visit to Washington at the end of July 2003, Bremer discovered that the reports he had been sending back to the Pentagon were not being shared with DOS, the CIA, or the White House. He felt that the entire interagency process had broken down. Frank Miller continued to gather information for Condoleezza Rice from the British, from the media, and through various military contacts, but no reporting was coming from Bremer. By August, Rice and Stephen Hadley felt that Rumsfeld had not been as involved with postwar Iraq as he had been with the war plan. Rice told Miller that it was not going well in Iraq and directed him to "[r]econstitute the ESG."[97]

In September, Bremer published an op-ed in the *Washington Post* that set out a seven-step plan for "Iraq's path to sovereignty." In it, he laid out a timetable for writing and ratifying a constitution and holding national elections as a prelude to the return of sovereignty. The article had not been approved by anyone in Washington, and his plan anticipated a longer transition process than some of the NSC principals thought desirable. Shortly after Bremer's op-ed was published, Rice made Blackwill her new coordinator for strategic planning on the NSC staff and assigned him to be the White House "point man" on Iraq.

On October 6, the *New York Times* ran the front-page headline "White House to Overhaul Iraq and Afghan Missions."[98] The article cited a leaked memo that called for Rice to replace Rumsfeld as the U.S. government's lead on Iraq and the creation of a new NSC organization, the Iraq Stabilization Group, to be headed by Blackwill. Bremer was surprised by the move. Rumsfeld was also caught off guard, first hearing of the change in a reporter's question while he was traveling outside Washington.

---

[95] Ricks (2006, p. 212).

[96] Bremer (2006a, pp. 168, 231).

[97] Woodward (2006, pp. 209, 212, 235–236, 240–241).

[98] David E. Sanger, "White House to Overhaul Iraq and Afghan Missions," *New York Times*, October 6, 2003.

While the Washington lead for Iraq policy was, indeed, to shift from DoD to the NSC staff, Bremer was still supposed to report to Rumsfeld.[99] Yet this, too, seemed less than clear. Following a meeting in the White House Situation Room, Rumsfeld and Rice argued over whom Bremer worked for. Rice told Rumsfeld that Bremer worked for him. Rumsfeld replied, "No, he doesn't. He's been talking to the NSC, he works for the NSC."[100]

In Rumsfeld's view, it would appear that, if Bremer were working for him, he would not be talking to the NSC staff. This position might be understandable if Bremer were a subordinate military commander, as these are indeed discouraged from communicating out of channels. But Bremer was a presidential envoy and a former ambassador. All U.S. ambassadors are personal representatives of the President and accustomed to maintaining lateral contacts with multiple government agencies, including the White House, while taking instructions from the Secretary of State.

Transition

On October 16, 2003, the UNSC, acting at U.S. behest, set a December 15 deadline for the IGC to submit a plan for drafting a constitution and electing a government. On November 15, Bremer returned from a trip to Washington and briefed the IGC on the new CPA transition plan, one much more rapid than that outlined in his *Washington Post* article two months earlier. The IGC complained that the United States was dictating rather than building consensus. The plan, which was also a surprise to CPA staff, marked a shift in the nexus of Iraq decisionmaking from Baghdad to Washington and set the following timetable:

- February 28, 2004: IGC to draft and approve the "transitional administrative law"
- March 31, 2004: CPA and IGC to ratify a status-of-forces agreement on coalition forces

---

[99] Bremer (2006a, p. 187).

[100] Ricks (2006, p. 181).

- May 31, 2004: local caucuses in 18 provinces to choose transitional national assembly that then would elect the transitional government to assume power by June 30
- June 30, 2004: CPA and IGC to be disestablished and the interim Iraqi government to be established
- June 30, 2004–December 31, 2005: interim Iraqi government in control
- March 15, 2005: direct national elections for constitutional convention
- December 31, 2005: national elections for a permanent Iraqi government.

The United States had been trying for months to get the UN to reengage in Iraq. In January 2004, Lakhdar Brahimi agreed to lead a technical mission to Iraq to assist in the transition to the new Iraqi government.[101]

Now that everyone agreed to return sovereignty to the Iraqi government no later than June 30, 2004, the Bush administration's attention shifted to what the U.S. presence in Iraq would look like following the transition. Powell and Rumsfeld argued over who would be in charge of nonmilitary U.S. personnel in Iraq. Powell insisted that, with the creation of the U.S. embassy in Baghdad, DOS through the ambassador would oversee the nonmilitary activities of the U.S. government. Rumsfeld insisted that DoD should remain in overall charge of the 130,000 troops still stationed there. Rice did not state her preference for one or the other but wanted the chain of command clearly delineated so that there would be no further arguments over who worked for whom. On May 11, 2004, President Bush signed NSPD 36, terminating the CPA no later than June 30 and in its place creating the U.S. Mission in Baghdad, which would be responsible for U.S. activities in Iraq.[102] NSPD 36 shifted responsibility from DoD to DOS, with one significant caveat: The chief of mission, or ambas-

---

[101] Diamond (2005, pp. 50–52, 136); Ricks (2006, p. 255).

[102] George W. Bush, National Security Presidential Directive 36, United States Government Operations in Iraq, May 11, 2004.

sador, would be "responsible for the direction, coordination and supervision of all United States government employees, policies and activities in country except those under the command of an area military commander."[103] Thus, the lines of authority in Iraq would return to those usually employed in postconflict environments, at least since the end of the German and Japanese occupations 50 years earlier.

On June 28, two days before the deadline and in secret due to security concerns, Bremer departed Iraq and the CPA ceased to exist. The United States established diplomatic relations with the Iraqi government. The entire CPA bureaucratic structure had to be dismantled and its functions handed back to Iraqi ministries or to the new embassy and its country team, creating some initial confusion as roles and missions were reassigned. The new ambassador, John Negroponte, and the new military commander, General George Casey, established a solid working relationship, but, after only six months, Negroponte left to become Director of National Intelligence. He was eventually replaced by Zalmay Khalilzad after a several-month gap with no ambassador in country.

The widespread looting and an almost complete breakdown in public order in Baghdad and elsewhere in the country following the disintegration of Saddam's regime soon gave way to mounting resistance to the U.S. occupation. With the transfer of sovereignty and then the national elections in 2005, the nature of the conflict mutated from national resistance to the U.S. presence to Sunni resistance to a Shia-dominated government. Shia militias (and Shia-dominated police) retaliated against Sunni attacks with atrocities of their own. Al Qaeda stoked the flames, attacking Shia targets precisely to stir such a response, thereby hoping to plunge the country further into chaos. Tens of thousands of Iraqis were killed, and millions were driven from their homes. Eventually, however, many Sunni leaders became disenchanted with al Qaeda's behavior and sought to ally with U.S. forces. By late 2007, an increase in U.S. troop strength, the U.S. military's adoption of increasingly sophisticated counterinsurgency tactics, and a more active U.S. diplomatic effort to engage neighboring governments

---

[103] Woodward (2006, p. 312).

had helped to reduce the violence, leading to an uneasy equilibrium among Kurdish, Sunni, and Shia factions, all of which were receiving some degree of support from the United States.

Improvements in Iraqi security were paralleled by improvements in interagency coordination in Washington. Robert Gates was chosen to succeed Donald Rumsfeld in November 2006. Gates, who had served as Brent Scowcroft's principal deputy in the George H. W. Bush administration, proved much more collegial in his approach to the policy process, working effectively with now–Secretary of State Rice across a range of issues. The White House also strengthened its own staffing, appointing a senior coordinator for both Iraq and Afghanistan, a position that had been filled only at a more junior level since Blackwill's departure from the administration in early 2005.

Conclusion

The Afghan campaign of 2001 provided a textbook illustration of the successful integration of force and diplomacy, of national power and international legitimacy.

In the weeks after 9/11, every agency of the U.S. government worked toward a common goal with minimal friction. The CIA ran paramilitary operations, DoD ran the military, and DOS handled the diplomacy. Each deferred to the other in its sphere of competence. The CIA put together the overall strategy for the war and guided the application of U.S. military power in support of a local insurgency. It put U.S. diplomats in contact with the key Afghan actors. The devastating effect of U.S. bombing gave decisive weight to U.S. diplomacy, and near-universal international support gave that diplomacy added influence. As a result, operating from a standing start, the United States was able to both displace the Taliban and replace it with a representative, moderate, domestically popular, and internationally recognized regime within three months.

Unfortunately, this harmony proved short lived. By late December 2001, the U.S. military presence in Afghanistan had grown from a few hundred to several thousand soldiers. Increasingly, the locus of decisionmaking on Afghanistan's future moved from the CIA and DOS to DoD. The Pentagon leadership determined that U.S. soldiers would not conduct peacekeeping, their usual postcombat role. On the other hand, U.S. troops would dispense humanitarian and reconstruction assistance, provide Hamid Karzai with a personal security detail, and build a new Afghan army, all functions that had been DOS responsibilities in previous nation-building missions. DoD had the money and the dominant presence on the ground, and its leadership had a clear idea about how the postcombat phase should be handled.

The speed and thoroughness of the U.S. victory in Afghanistan demonstrated how much could be achieved when all elements of the U.S. government operated in harmony with the international community, and particularly with the neighboring and regional powers most likely to have influence. This was not the lesson drawn by the administration, however, nor, truth be told, by Congress or the American people. Few Americans recognized the nature of the international coalition that had toppled the Taliban regime or the importance of regional actors in helping establish its successor. Rather, the dominant impression left by the rapid victory of U.S. forces in 2001 was one of near omnipotence.

When the focus of attention in Washington turned to Iraq, the synergy achieved by fully harnessing CIA, DoD, and DOS capabilities was not sustained. In Iraq, all civil and military functions would be performed under the direction of the Secretary of Defense. DOS and the CIA would be called upon to deploy personnel and assist on the ground, but they were not effectively incorporated into the design of postwar policy in Washington. Neither, rather remarkably, was the White House.

The result was a campaign in Iraq that forwent nearly all the advantages of interagency and international collaboration that had delivered such rapid success in Afghanistan. The conventional military victory was still impressive, but the political and economic follow-through ran into immediate difficulties. If the Afghan campaign of late 2001 showed how much the United States could achieve with interagency collaboration and international support, developments in Iraq soon illustrated how little could be accomplished without them.

What role did style, structure, and process play in these initial missteps? In the light of hindsight, one can identify a number of critical decisions made by President Bush and his advisers that would likely have been improved had there been more methodical interagency debate. Chief among these was the decision to invade Iraq in the first place, which does not seem to have been exposed to such a process. Former CIA Director George Tenet, in his memoirs, asserts that the wisdom of doing so was never discussed among NSC principals. Donald Rumsfeld has admitted to *Washington Post* journalist Bob Woodward that President Bush never asked his opinion on the subject. Colin Powell raised his reservations with the President by his own initiative, but these concerns were never subjected to serious interagency examination.

Early policy regarding Afghanistan's stabilization and reconstruction, however inadequate it ultimately proved, did emerge from an orderly and inclusive interagency process. In contrast, many of the most important decisions with respect to Iraq, beginning with that to invade, were not subjected to any such structured debate. For months after Bremer's arrival in Baghdad, DoD did not share CPA communications with DOS, the CIA, or the White House. As time wore on, even DoD's oversight attenuated, with Rumsfeld eventually insisting to Rice that Bremer was now working for her rather than him. It was during this period of maximum confusion over lines of authority that Bremer published a timetable for the restoration of sovereignty that had not been approved by any of the NSC principals.

As a practical matter, from the time President Bush assigned overall responsibility for postwar planning to the Pentagon until the moment Condoleezza Rice charged Robert Blackwill with taking charge of Iraq policy, it seems that the Washington-based interagency process for Iraq had largely ceased to function. The idea that such a process could be transferred from Washington to Baghdad seems, in hindsight, highly unrealistic. From the day of his arrival, Bremer and his top lieutenants were overwhelmed by the responsibilities for governing and rebuilding a badly divided nation that was rapidly sinking into chaos. They had little time for reflection, no capacity to study or research complex issues, and no organizational memory regarding prior U.S. or international endeavors of this nature. At the mid- and junior levels, the CPA was scantly staffed by people with only limited relevant experience, most of whom stayed no more that a few months. Neither could Bremer's senior staff necessarily speak for the agencies that sent them. DOS, the Treasury Department, and the CIA sent small numbers of well-qualified officials to Baghdad, but none was of cabinet or subcabinet rank. Communication with Washington was limited, making it difficult for agencies to backstop their forward personnel and for those individuals to keep their home offices well informed.

The allegation that the Bush administration did not conduct any postwar planning for Iraq is overstated. As Jay Garner noted,

> Defense had done a lot of planning. State had done a lot of planning. USAID had done an awful lot of planning. Agriculture had done planning. Treasury had done an awful lot of planning. Justice Department had done an awful lot of planning. Each one of them did their own planning, and they did it with the perspective of their agency.[104]

What was missing was the effective integration of these many plans. In effect, the hard-learned process lessons of the 1990s embodied in PDD 56 were unlearned in the early days of the Bush administration.

The most crippling consequence of the lack of formalized interagency planning was the absence of a plan B, if any of the assumptions underpinning the administration's postwar intentions proved ill founded. Much of the postwar planning was conducted under the conviction that Iraq's army would capitulate virtually in toto and that the Iraqi police had adequate professional training and were not closely tied to the Saddam Hussein regime.[105] It was therefore assumed that both these forces would be available to help the coalition secure Iraq after the fall of the regime. Similarly, the postwar planners consistently underestimated how bad conditions were inside Iraq. After returning to the United States, Bremer noted, "The information we had about the

---

[104]In Fineman, Wright, and McManus (2003).

[105]On the CIA estimates of the Iraqi army and police, see Gordon and Trainor (2006, pp. 105, 161, 165).

state of the Iraqi economy was not good. The economy was in much worse shape than I had been led to believe."[106] Major General Carl Strock, who came to ORHA by way of the Army Corps of Engineers, recalled, "We sort of made the assumption that the country was functioning beforehand. I had a dramatic underestimation of the condition of the Iraqi infrastructure, which turned out to be one of our biggest problems."[107] Again, the fundamental problem was not the content of these particular assumptions, each of which was defensible on its own terms. The problem was that no alternate set of assumptions was incorporated into the Bush administration's planning efforts, and no contingency plans were developed in case the desired scenario did not occur.[108]

While all nation-building efforts have been plagued by problems of interagency coordination to one degree or another, the cure chosen by the Bush administration, reposing all authority with the Secretary of Defense, turned out to be considerably worse than the disease. By transferring plenary responsibility for postwar Iraq to one cabinet department, the President effectively took himself and his staff out of the loop. Yet the U.S. effort in Iraq remained divided between military and civilian lines of authority.

DOS, while lacking DoD's size and budget, does have extensive experience opening and operating branch offices of the U.S. government abroad. U.S. diplomatic missions have functioned alongside U.S. armed forces in Korea, Vietnam, the Dominican Republic, Lebanon, Grenada, Panama, Somalia, Haiti, Bosnia, Kosovo, and Afghanistan—that is to say, throughout every international conflict of the past 50 years. Other agencies are familiar with this arrangement and know how they fit into it. Prenegotiated provisions cover who pays for what, how far the chief of mission's authority extends over the activities of other agency representatives, and who is responsible for what functions. Communication procedures are familiar, and reporting is

---

[106] L. Paul Bremer III, *Frontline*, edited interview transcript, June 26 and August 18, 2006b.

[107] In Gordon and Trainor (2006, p. 150).

[108] Bensahel (2006, p. 458).

widely and routinely shared. All this had to be reinvented in setting up the CPA, a unique and unprecedented civilian mission abroad run by a different agency.

President Bush's management style emphasized inspiration and guidance from above and loyalty and compliance from below. In such an atmosphere, individuals within the system who doubted the wisdom of invading Iraq or the adequacy of plans to stabilize and rebuild both Afghanistan and Iraq were not encouraged to articulate those concerns. By adopting such a top-down approach to decisionmaking, the President denied himself the more carefully considered proposals, better analysis, and more thorough planning that a dialectical process of structured debate would have produced. Condoleezza Rice has been criticized for not having imposed a more rigorous interagency process on her older and seasoned colleagues on the NSC/PC. It seems likely, however, that President Bush got the NSC process he desired.

In early 2007, President Bush acted contrarily to the initial recommendations of many of his senior civilian and military advisers and significantly increased the U.S. troop strength in Iraq. In this instance, Bush does seem to have consulted widely both within and outside the NSC, giving all the major stakeholders an opportunity to express their views. Neither the JCS nor the Secretary of State initially favored the move. Bush spent two hours discussing the issue with the former. He also reviewed the options with the rest of his national security team. "Though Bush had all but decided on a surge before the formal 'interagency review' began," wrote Fred Barnes in the *Weekly Standard*, "the process wasn't a charade. It forced the president to consider alternatives. And it also involved agencies besides the White House—the Defense and State departments, the CIA, the Joint Chiefs. 'At a very minimum,' the president said, it made them 'feel they had a say in the development of a strategy.'"[109]

Whether this more comprehensive and methodical process of consultation was the result of experience or simply the product of the President's weakened political position is unclear. In any case, the surge in troop levels, in conjunction with other factors, resulted in a sig-

---

[109] Fred Barnes, "How Bush Decided on the Surge," *Weekly Standard*, February 4, 2008.

nificant reduction in violence in Iraq. This experience illustrates that, while a president need not do what advisers recommend, he or she will make better decisions and get more wholehearted support for their implementation if they are consulted beforehand.

CHAPTER SIX

Toward Better Decisions and More Competent Execution

Successful nation-building requires unity of effort across multiple agencies and, often, multiple governments. Decisionmaking structures thus need to provide for a combination of common effort and unified direction. The requirement to include not just other agencies but also other governments and international organizations in modern nation-building enterprises makes any replication of the MacArthur viceroy model unrealistic. The entire U.S. national security establishment needs to be engaged, as does much of the international community. This is not a responsibility that presidents can afford to delegate, nor one that any single department of government can handle.

Decisionmaking structures thus need to reflect an appropriate balance between a well-structured, deliberative process and the varying styles of any individual president. The Clinton-era PDD 56 provides one possible template. However much it was praised during that administration, the process as outlined therein at least gave guidance to what "right" decisionmaking would look like.

The key element of any process is a senior IWG that includes all relevant agencies. This will generally mean, at a minimum, DoD and DOS, along with the CIA (in an advisory rather than policymaking capacity, though clearly the line between the two is seldom distinct). This working group will provide a forum for the airing of divergent views and should be tasked with creating a range of options and likely scenarios. Members should be allowed significant latitude to disagree in this initial period. In effect, this is an attempt to institutionalize the collegial model of decisionmaking at the working level of the executive branch.

Of particular importance is the collegial model's emphasis on lateral communication. Unfortunately, this is often easier said than done and can depend heavily on the personalities involved. Parochial feelings can often limit the willingness and ability to communicate laterally. Attempting to implement a certain level of interagency comfort is probably required to make this communication work. One possible way to foster this is to require cross- or interagency tours for all those seeking senior positions within civilian agencies, much as the military services require a joint assignment for promotion. While this will not solve everything, it will act to expose, for example, DOS personnel to the culture and workings of DoD and vice versa.

Once an option is selected, a fully integrated political-military plan should be generated. This is tricky, because the same type of interagency group that was given free range to develop and dissent over options must now be tasked with executing a single option. This may be an option to which some were strenuously opposed in the initial phase of decisionmaking. Regardless, it is important that all relevant players be included in implementation planning.

This political-military integration includes having civilian agencies give advice on war plans to the military and vice versa. This will undoubtedly be painful; the military doubtless does not want to hear USAID's view on target selection any more than USAID wants to hear the military's view on the utility of public-works projects in combat zones. However, advice does not equal final authority; serious disputes will have to be aired and resolved by senior leaders, including the president, if necessary. It is better that such disputes be ironed out before nation-building begins rather than in the middle of an operation. Such integration has been muddled in almost all post–World War II efforts, so any serious attempt to improve the process must address this problem.

While integrated political-military planning is important, so is establishing a clear and enduring division of labor for various aspects of nation-building. It is a bureaucratic truism that, "when all are responsible for an issue, none takes responsibility." In other words, lack of clear responsibility for an issue is a recipe for buck-passing and indecision.

For the past 15 years, critical functions, such as overseeing military and police training, providing humanitarian and reconstruction aid, and promoting democratic development, have been repeatedly transferred from DOS to DoD and back again. This has left each agency uncertain about what its long-term responsibilities are and consequently disinclined to invest in improving its performance. Only a division of labor established in legislation is likely to endure from one president to the next and will thus give the respective agencies assurance regarding their roles and promote long-term investment.

The United States must decide whether nation-building is going to be an enduring part of its repertoire of national security activities. If so, it must rebalance the political and military elements of national power. For example, the Army and Marine Corps are projected to add about 90,000 troops over the next several years. Despite recent and projected future expansions, the total number of personnel in civilian agencies associated with nation-building, including USAID, the CIA, and DOS, is dwarfed by this number. Budgets are similarly weighted toward the military. Absent some effort to redress this imbalance and to create an operational civilian cadre for nation-building, the implementation of U.S. nation-building policy is likely to remain stunted no matter how good the quality of its decisionmaking.

If DOS and USAID are to receive more funding and personnel to perform these functions, those personnel will need to be available when required. It is not realistic to think that domestic civil servants can be sent involuntarily into a war zone. Foreign Service personnel, however, are already subject, in theory at least, to worldwide availability. This practice of directed assignments has largely lapsed since thousands of DOS and USAID officers were sent to Vietnam. It will have to be revitalized if these agencies are to secure and retain the higher funding and personnel levels that their nation-building responsibilities require.

It should be no surprise that administrations get better at policy formulation and execution as they progress. Neither should it be surprising that much of this acquired experience is not passed on from one administration to the next, particularly when the successor is of an opposing party. Nevertheless, the degree to which the U.S. government has experienced a regression in competence in the field of nation-building from one administration to the next should be a source of concern. Obstacles to the transmission of expertise should be identified and, where possible, leveled.

Two modern administrations that are often held up as exemplars of orderly process and sound policy under exceptionally challenging circumstances are those of Harry Truman and George H. W. Bush. Both had been vice presidents and had extensive Washington experience. Truman took office at the opening of the Cold War, in the 13th year of a Democratic administration, and retained in one capacity or another many on his predecessor's national security team. Bush succeeded Ronald Reagan, also a Republican. Neither Truman nor the elder Bush had campaigned against his predecessor's record, and neither administration felt obligated to do things differently simply to disassociate itself from what had come before. The quality of both presidencies profited from this continuity of personnel and policy.

Bill Clinton and George W. Bush, by contrast, had no Washington experience, and both wished to emphasize discontinuity with their predecessors. Many of their advisers felt even more strongly the need to do so. These advisers had Washington experience, but it was dated, the world having changed dramatically while their parties were out of power. Clinton faltered immediately in Somalia. Bush did well at first in Afghanistan but did not sustain that success in Iraq or, for that matter, in Afghanistan.

Alternance in power is, of course, an essential condition and necessary product of democracy. Frequent elections, the two-party system, and presidential term limits are designed to produce benefits that transcend technical competence in the design and implementation of foreign policy. Passage of the 22nd Amendment of the Constitution in the aftermath of President Roosevelt's successful conduct of World War II represented, in fact, a rather explicit national choice in favor of innovation over expertise. In the U.S. political system, however, the costs and risks associated with such transitions are magnified by the scale of its patronage system, the scope of which is unparalleled in the Western world. The United States' reliance on the spoils system to empty and fill thousands of high- and medium-level policy positions every four, eight, or 12 years ensures a high degree of inexperience in the opening years of many presidencies and promotes strong barriers to continuity of policy from one administration to the next. It also results in diminished competence in a civil service whose members are denied access to positions of greater responsibility. Heavy reliance on patronage to fill key staff positions effectively insulates political leaders at the top from professional advice at the bottom, imposing several layers of ideological buffer between the two. This problem has become more acute in recent decades as the number of positions in the national security establishment subject to partisan selection has risen.

It is unrealistic to think that a country as large, varied, and dynamic as the United States could be governed through a civil service of elite mandarins on the basis of British, French, or German models. Nevertheless, Congress has largely walled off the U.S. military, law-enforcement, and intelligence services from patronage appointments on the grounds that public security is too important to be politicized. Setting aside some proportion of subcabinet and White House staff positions in the national security arena for career personnel could be similarly justified and would go far to diminish the turbulence associated with changes in administrations, thereby reducing the alarming incidence of neophyte presidents making flawed decisions on the advice of loyal but inadequately experienced staff.

Setbacks in Iraq and a sense that U.S. leadership is faltering worldwide has led some to argue that the entire interagency structure first given form in 1947 is outdated. The world, it is argued, is a far more complex place today, and the U.S. government is much larger. In fact, however, the world is not more complex today than it was in 1947, and the federal government is not all that much larger. One has only to recall the incredible turbulence that affected the international system in the decade after World War II, with the fall of the Iron Curtain, the "loss" of China, and the disintegration of the British and French colonial empires, to put today's challenges into perspective. It is true that information moves much more quickly today, and the federal government has many more civilian employees and fewer military personnel than it did 60 years ago. Neither of these factors necessarily makes policy harder to formulate and execute.

In fact, the current system for integrating defense and foreign policy has actually functioned quite well for most of the past 60 years. It helped win the Cold War, unite Europe, cope with the collapse of the Soviet Union, deal with the early challenges of the post–Cold War era, and initially respond to the attacks of 9/11. A system that was working adequately only six years ago is probably not irretrievably broken. As this monograph has illustrated, many of what are now widely considered to be flawed decisions of the past several years were made not because the interagency system was defective but because it was circumvented or neglected.

That said, there are improvements that would strengthen the capacity of the current system to deal successfully with the intense interagency and international integration required for successful nation-building. Legislation to establish an enduring division of labor among DOS, DoD, USAID, and other agencies engaged in these missions would promote the development of a more professional approach to nation-building, as would a provision to require a tour of service in a national security agency other than one's own for entry into the senior executive staff or foreign service. Legislation to set aside a certain proportion of subcabinet and White House staff positions for career officers would also help sustain the learning curve from one administration to the next.

Whatever management style presidents may adopt—formal, competitive, collegial, or some combination—it is important that they foster debate among their principal advisers and value disciplined dissent as an essential aid to wise decisionmaking. It is equally important that presidents and their principal advisers have access to professional, experienced staff. Once decisions are made, these need to be implemented, to the extent possible, through established structures, employing tried methodologies and respecting existing lines of authority. Most bureaucratic innovation comes at significant cost in terms of immediately degraded performance, whatever its long-term effect. Institutional improvisation may be necessary to cope with new challenges. Nation-building, however, is a familiar and repetitive requirement—one that requires greater consistency of method and transmission of expertise from one administration to the next than the system has thus far achieved.

Bibliography

Allison, Graham, and Philip Zelikow, *Essence of Decision: Explaining the Cuban Missile Crisis*, 2nd ed., New York: Longman, 1999.

Ash, Timothy Garton, "Kosovo: Was It Worth It?" *New York Review of Books*, Vol. 47, No. 14, September 21, 2000.

Barnes, Fred, "How Bush Decided on the Surge," *Weekly Standard*, February 4, 2008. As of April 7, 2008:
http://www.weeklystandard.com/Content/Public/Articles/000/000/014/658dwgrn.asp

Bensahel, Nora, "Mission Not Accomplished: What Went Wrong with Iraqi Reconstruction," *Journal of Strategic Studies*, Vol. 29, No. 3, June 2006, pp. 453–473.

Beschloss, Michael, *The Conquerors: Roosevelt, Truman and the Destruction of Hitler's Germany, 1941–1945*, New York: Simon and Schuster, 2002.

Borton, Hugh, "Presuppositions, Prejudices, and Planning," in Robert Wolfe, ed., *Americans as Proconsuls: United States Military Government in Germany and Japan, 1944–1952*, Carbondale, Ill.: Southern Illinois University Press, 1984, pp. 1–2.

Bowden, Mark, *Black Hawk Down: A Story of Modern War*, Berkeley, Calif.: Atlantic Monthly Press, 1999.

Bremer, L. Paul III, with Malcolm McConnell, *My Year in Iraq: The Struggle to Build a Future of Hope*, New York: Simon and Schuster, 2006a.

———, *Frontline*, edited interview transcript, June 26 and August 18, 2006b.

———, "How I Didn't Dismantle Iraq's Army," *New York Times*, September 6, 2007, p. 27.

Bucci, Steven P., *Complex Contingencies: Presidential Decision Directive 56: The Case of Kosovo and the Future*, Arlington, Va.: National Foreign Affairs Training Center, undated.

Bush, George H. W., National Security Directive 1, Organization of the National Security Council System, Washington, D.C.: White House, January 30, 1989. As of April 7, 2008:
http://bushlibrary.tamu.edu/research/pdfs/nsd/nsd1.pdf

Bush, George W., National Security Presidential Directive 1, Organization of the National Security Council System, Washington, D.C.: White House, February 13, 2001. As of April 7, 2008:
http://fas.org/irp/offdocs/nspd/nspd-1.htm

————, National Security Presidential Directive 24, on postwar Iraq reconstruction, Washington, D.C.: White House, January 20, 2003.

————, National Security Presidential Directive 36, United States Government Operations in Iraq, May 11, 2004. As of April 7, 2008:
http://www.fas.org/irp/offdocs/nspd/nspd051104.pdf

————, National Security Presidential Directive 44, Management of Interagency Efforts Concerning Reconstruction and Stabilization, Washington, D.C.: White House, December 7, 2005. As of April 7, 2008:
http://www.fas.org/irp/offdocs/nspd/nspd-44.html

Cairo Communiqué, December 1, 1943. As of April 7, 2008:
http://www.ndl.go.jp/constitution/e/shiryo/01/002_46shoshi.html

Clark, Wesley K., *Waging Modern War: Bosnia, Kosovo, and the Future of Combat*, New York: Public Affairs, 2001.

Clinton, William J., Presidential Decision Directive 2, Organization of the National Security Council, Washington, D.C.: White House, January 20, 1993a. As of April 7, 2008:
http://fas.org/irp/offdocs/pdd/pdd-2.htm

————, Presidential Review Directive 13, Peacekeeping Operations, February 1993b. Not available to the general public.

————, Presidential Decision Directive 25, U.S. Policy on Reforming Multilateral Peace Operations, May 3, 1994.

————, *My Life*, New York: Alfred A. Knopf, 2004.

Coalition Provisional Authority Order Number 1, De-Ba'athification of Iraqi Society, May 16, 2003. As of April 7, 2008:
http://www.cpa-iraq.org/regulations/20030516_CPAORD_1_De-Ba_athification_of_Iraqi_Society_.pdf

Coalition Provisional Authority Order Number 2, Dissolution of Entities, May 23, 2003. As of April 7, 2008:
http://www.cpa-iraq.org/regulations/20030823_CPAORD_2_Dissolution_of_Entities_with_Annex_A.pdf

Cohen, Theodore, *Remaking Japan: The American Occupation as New Deal*, Herbert Passin, ed., New York: Free Press, 1987.

Collins, Joseph J., "Planning Lessons from Afghanistan and Iraq," *Joint Forces Quarterly*, No. 41, 2nd Quarter 2006, pp. 10–14. As of April 7, 2008: http://www.dtic.mil/doctrine/jel/jfq_pubs/4105.pdf

Cronin, Richard P., *Afghanistan: Challenges and Options for Reconstructing a Stable and Moderate State*, CRS Report for Congress, Washington, D.C.: Congressional Research Service, April 24, 2002.

Cusimano, Maryann K., *Operation Restore Hope: The Bush Administration's Decision to Intervene in Somalia*, Washington, D.C.: Institute for the Study of Diplomacy, 1995.

Daalder, Ivo H., *The Clinton Administration and Multilateral Peace Operations*, Washington, D.C.: Institute for the Study of Diplomacy, 1994.

———, *Getting to Dayton: The Making of America's Bosnia Policy*, Washington, D.C.: Brookings Institution Press, 2000.

Daalder, Ivo H., and I. M. Destler, "The Bush Administration National Security Council," *The National Security Council Project: Oral History Roundtables*, Washington, D.C.: Brookings Institution, April 29, 1999.

———, "The Clinton Administration National Security Council," *The National Security Council Project: Oral History Roundtables*, Washington, D.C.: Brookings Institution, September 27, 2000.

Daalder, Ivo H., and Michael E. O'Hanlon, *Winning Ugly: NATO's War to Save Kosovo*, Washington, D.C.: Brookings Institution Press, 2000.

DeLong, Michael, and Noah Lukeman, *Inside CENTCOM: the Unvarnished Truth About the Wars in Afghanistan and Iraq*, Washington, D.C.: Regnery Publishing, 2004.

Diamond, Larry, *Squandered Victory: The American Occupation and the Bungled Effort to Bring Democracy to Iraq*, New York: Times Books, 2005.

Dobbins, James, Seth G. Jones, Keith Crane, and Beth Cole DeGrasse, *The Beginner's Guide to Nation-Building*, Santa Monica, Calif.: RAND Corporation, MG-557-SRF, 2007. As of April 4, 2008: http://www.rand.org/pubs/monographs/MG557/

Dobbins, James, Seth G. Jones, Keith Crane, Andrew Rathmell, Brett Steele, Richard Teltschik, and Anga R. Timilsina, *The UN's Role in Nation-Building: From the Congo to Iraq*, Santa Monica, Calif.: RAND Corporation, MG-304-RC, 2005. As of April 4, 2008: http://www.rand.org/pubs/monographs/MG304/

Dobbins, James, John G. McGinn, Keith Crane, Seth G. Jones, Rollie Lal, Andrew Rathmell, Rachel M. Swanger, and Anga R. Timilsina, *America's Role in Nation-Building: From Germany to Iraq*, Santa Monica, Calif.: RAND Corporation, MR-1753-RC, 2003. As of April 4, 2008: http://www.rand.org/pubs/monograph_reports/MR1753/

Fallows, James, "Blind into Baghdad," *Atlantic Monthly*, January–February 2004. As of April 7, 2008: http://www.theatlantic.com/doc/200401/fallows

Fineman, Mark, Robin Wright, and Doyle McManus, "Preparing for War, Stumbling to Peace," *Los Angeles Times*, July 18, 2003.

Flournoy, Michèle, "Interagency Strategy and Planning for Post-Conflict Reconstruction," in Robert C. Orr, ed., *Winning the Peace: An American Strategy for Post-Conflict Reconstruction*, Washington, D.C.: CSIS Press, 2004, pp. 105–115.

Franks, Tommy, with Malcolm McConnell, *American Soldier*, New York: Regan Books, 2004.

Fukuyama, Francis, *The End of History and the Last Man*, New York: Free Press, 1992.

———, "Introduction: Nation-Building and the Failure of Institutional Memory," in Francis Fukuyama, ed., *Nation-Building: Beyond Afghanistan and Iraq*, Baltimore, Md.: Johns Hopkins University Press, 2006, pp. 1–16.

Garner, Lieutenant General Jay, *Frontline*, interview transcript, July 17, 2003. As of April 7, 2008: http://www.pbs.org/wgbh/pages/frontline/shows/truth/interviews/garner.html

———, *Frontline*, interview transcript, August 11, 2006. As of April 7, 2008: http://www.pbs.org/wgbh/pages/frontline/yeariniraq/interviews/garner.html

George, Alexander L., *Presidential Decisionmaking in Foreign Policy: The Effective Use of Information and Advice*, Boulder, Colo.: Westview Press, 1980.

George, Alexander L., and Eric Stern, "Presidential Management Styles and Models," in Alexander L. George and Juliette L. George, eds., *Presidential Personality and Performance*, Boulder, Colo.: Westview Press, 1998, pp. 199–280.

Gimbel, John, "Governing the American Zone in Germany," in Robert Wolfe, ed., *Americans as Proconsuls: United States Military Government in Germany and Japan, 1944–1952*, Carbondale, Ill.: Southern Illinois University Press, 1984, pp. 92–102.

Goodson, Larry P., "The Lessons of Nation-Building in Afghanistan," in Francis Fukuyama, ed., *Nation-Building: Beyond Afghanistan and Iraq*, Baltimore, Md.: Johns Hopkins University Press, 2006, pp. 145–171.

Gordon, Michael R., "The Strategy to Secure Iraq Did Not Foresee a 2nd War," *New York Times*, October 19, 2004, p. A1.

Gordon, Michael R., and Bernard E. Trainor, *Cobra II: The Inside Story of the Invasion and Occupation of Iraq*, New York: Pantheon Books, 2006.

Hayes, Margaret Daly, and Gary F. Wheatley, eds., *Interagency and Political-Military Dimensions of Peace Operations: Haiti—A Case Study*, Washington, D.C.: National Defense University, 1996. As of April 7, 2008:
http://handle.dtic.mil/100.2/ADA310900

Hersh, Seymour, "Selective Intelligence," *New Yorker*, May 12, 2003. As of April 7, 2008:
http://www.newyorker.com/archive/2003/05/12/030512fa_fact

Hess, Stephen, and James P. Pfiffner, *Organizing the Presidency*, 3rd ed., Washington, D.C.: Brookings Institution Press, 2002.

Holbrooke, Richard, *To End a War*, New York: Modern Library, 1999.

Huntington, Samuel, *Clash of Civilizations and the Remaking of World Order*, New York: Simon and Schuster, 1996.

Ignatieff, Michael, "Chains of Command," *New York Review of Books*, Vol. 48, No. 12, July 19, 2001.

Institute for National Strategic Studies, National Defense University, *Improving the Utility of Presidential Decision Directive 56: A Plan of Action for the Joint Chiefs of Staff*, Washington, D.C., March 1999.

Janis, Irving L., *Groupthink: Psychological Studies of Policy Decisions and Fiascos*, 2nd ed., Boston, Mass.: Houghton Mifflin, 1982.

Janis, Irving L., and Leon Mann, *Decision Making: A Psychological Analysis of Conflict, Choice, and Commitment,* New York: Free Press, 1977.

Johnson, Richard, *Managing the White House*, New York: Harper and Row, 1974.

Joint Chiefs of Staff Directive 1067, Directive to Commander-in-Chief of United States Forces of Occupation Regarding the Military Government in Germany, April 1945.

Joint Chiefs of Staff Directive 1380, Basic Directive for Post-Surrender Military Government in Japan Proper, November 1945.

Joulwan, George A., and Christopher C. Shoemaker, *Civilian-Military Cooperation in the Prevention of Deadly Conflict: Implementing the Agreements in Bosnia and Beyond*, New York: Carnegie Corporation, December 1995. As of April 7, 2008:
http://handle.dtic.mil/100.2/ADA372329

Katzman, Kenneth, *Afghanistan: Post-War Governance, Security, and U.S. Policy*, CRS Report for Congress, Washington, D.C.: Congressional Research Service, November 3, 2006.

Kennedy, John F., "Foreword," in Theodore Sorenson, *Decision-Making in the White House: The Olive Branch and the Arrows*, 2nd ed., New York: Columbia University Press, [1963] 2005, pp. xxix–xxxi.

Kim, Julie, *Bosnia: Overview of Issues Ten Years After Dayton*, CRS Report for Congress, Washington, D.C.: Congressional Research Service, November 14, 2005. As of April 7, 2008:
http://fpc.state.gov/documents/organization/57459.pdf

Kretchik, Walter E., Robert F. Baumann, and John T. Fishel, *Invasion, Intervention, "Intervasion": A Concise History of the U.S. Army in Operation Uphold Democracy*, Ft. Leavenworth, Kan.: U.S. Army Command and General Staff College Press, 1998.

Lake, Tony, and General Wesley Clark, "Reforming Multilateral Peace Operations (PDD 25) Press Briefing," Washington, D.C.: White House, May 5, 1994. As of April 7, 2008:
http://www.fas.org/irp/offdocs/pdd25_brief.htm

Martin, Curtis H., *President Clinton's Haiti Dilemma: Trial by Failure*, Washington, D.C.: Institute for the Study of Diplomacy, 1997.

Mayo, Marlene J., "American Wartime Planning for Occupied Japan: The Role of the Experts," in Robert Wolfe, ed., *Americans as Proconsuls: United States Military Government in Germany and Japan, 1944–1952*, Carbondale, Ill.: Southern Illinois University Press, 1984, pp. 3–51.

Menkhaus, Ken, and Louis Ortmayer, *Key Decisions in the Somalia Intervention*, Washington, D.C.: Institute for the Study of Diplomacy, 1995.

National Security Council Deputies Committee, *Mission Analysis: International Provisional Administration (IPA) for Kosovo*, draft staff assessment, 1999.

Near East South Asia Center for Strategic Studies, National Defense University, "Pre-War Planning for Post-War Iraq," undated. As of April 7, 2008:
http://www.au.af.mil/au/awc/awcgate/dod/postwar_iraq.htm

Newsom, David, "Background Press Brief on Kosovo IPA," U.S. Department of State, June 11, 1999.

Oliker, Olga, Richard Kauzlarich, James Dobbins, Kurt W. Basseuner, Donald L. Sampler, John G. McGinn, Michael J. Dziedzic, Adam Grissom, Bruce L. Pirnie, Nora Bensahel, and A. Isar Guven, *Aid During Conflict: Interaction Between Military and Civilian Assistance Providers in Afghanistan, September 2001–June 2002*, Santa Monica, Calif.: RAND Corporation, MG-212-OSD, 2004. As of April 7, 2008:
http://www.rand.org/pubs/monographs/MG212/

O'Sullivan, Christopher D., *Sumner Welles, Postwar Planning, and the Quest for a New World Order, 1937–1943*, New York: Columbia University Press, 2003. As of April 4, 2008:
http://www.gutenberg-e.org/osc01/

Packer, George, *The Assassins' Gate: America in Iraq*, New York: Farrar, Straus and Giroux, 2005.

Peterson, LTC Steven W., "Central but Inadequate: The Application of Theory in Operation Iraqi Freedom," thesis, National Defense University, 2004. As of April 7, 2008:
http://handle.dtic.mil/100.2/ADA441663

Phillips, David, *Losing Iraq*, Boulder, Colo.: Westview Press, 2005.

Presidential Decision Directive 56, Managing Complex Contingency Operations, May 1997.

Public Law 80-235, National Security Act of 1947, July 26, 1947.

Public Law 107-327, Afghanistan Freedom Support Act of 2002, December 4, 2002.

Ricks, Thomas E., *Fiasco: The American Military Adventure in Iraq*, New York: Penguin, 2006.

Rieff, David, "Blueprint for a Mess," *New York Times Magazine*, November 2, 2003. As of April 7, 2008:
http://www.nytimes.com/2003/11/02/magazine/02IRAQ.html

Roan, Richard, Erik Kjonnerod, and Robert Oakley, "Dealing with Complex Contingencies," Institute for National Strategic Studies Transition Papers, Washington, D.C.: National Defense University, December 21, 2000.

Rothkopf, David J., *Running the World: The Inside Story of the National Security Council and the Architects of American Power*, New York: Public Affairs, 2005.

Rubin, Michael, "Iraq in Books: Review Essay," *Middle East Quarterly*, Vol. 14, No. 2, Spring 2007, pp. 17–39.

Sanger, David E., "White House to Overhaul Iraq and Afghan Missions," *New York Times*, October 6, 2003, p. 1.

Scarborough, Rowan, "Pentagon Policy-Makers Battle Waning Morale," *Washington Times*, August 12, 2002.

Schonberger, Howard B., *Aftermath of War: Americans and the Remaking of Japan, 1945–1952*, Kent, Ohio: Kent State University Press, 1989.

Schmitt, Eric, and Joel Brinkley, "State Dept. Study Foresaw Trouble Now Plaguing Iraq," *New York Times*, October 19, 2003, p. 1.

Senor, Dan, and Walter Slocombe, "Too Few Good Men," *New York Times*, November 17, 2005, p. A31.

Sheehan, John J., "Why I Declined to Serve," *Washington Post*, April 16, 2007.

Slocombe, Walter B., "To Build an Army," *Washington Post*, November 5, 2003, p. A29.

Starr, S. Frederick, "Sovereignty and Legitimacy in Afghan Nation-Building," in Francis Fukuyama, ed., *Nation-Building: Beyond Afghanistan and Iraq*, Baltimore, Md.: Johns Hopkins University Press, 2006, pp. 107–124.

State-War-Navy Coordinating Committee Directive 150, Politico-Military Problems in the Far East: United States Initial Post-Defeat Policy Relating to Japan, September 1945.

United Nations Security Council Resolution 794, on the situation in Somalia, December 3, 1992. As of April 7, 2008:
http://daccessdds.un.org/doc/UNDOC/GEN/N92/772/11/PDF/N9277211.pdf?
OpenElement

United Nations Security Council Resolution 837, on the situation in Somalia, June 6, 1993. As of April 7, 2008:
http://daccessdds.un.org/doc/UNDOC/GEN/N93/332/32/IMG/N9333232.pdf?
OpenElement

United Nations Security Council Resolution 940, on authorization to form a multinational force under unified command and control to restore the legitimately elected president and authorities of the government of Haiti and extensions of the mandate of the UN Mission in Haiti, July 31, 1994. As of April 7, 2008:
http://daccessdds.un.org/doc/UNDOC/GEN/N94/312/22/PDF/N9431222.pdf?
OpenElement

United Nations Security Council Resolution 975, on extension of the mandate of the UN Mission in Haiti and transfer of responsibility from the multinational force in Haiti to the UN Mission in Haiti, January 30, 1995. As of April 7, 2008:
http://daccessdds.un.org/doc/UNDOC/GEN/N95/028/26/PDF/N9502826.pdf?
OpenElement

United Nations Security Council Resolution 1244, on the situation in Kosovo, June 10, 1999. As of April 7, 2008:
http://daccessdds.un.org/doc/UNDOC/GEN/N99/172/89/PDF/N9917289.pdf?
OpenElement

United Nations Security Council Resolution 1378, on the situation in Afghanistan, November 14, 2001. As of April 7, 2008:
http://daccessdds.un.org/doc/UNDOC/GEN/N01/638/57/PDF/N0163857.pdf?
OpenElement

United Nations Security Council Resolution 1383, on the situation in Afghanistan, December 6, 2001. As of April 7, 2008:
http://daccessdds.un.org/doc/UNDOC/GEN/N01/681/09/PDF/N0168109.pdf?
OpenElement

United Nations Security Council Resolution 1401, on the situation in Afghanistan, March 28, 2002. As of April 7, 2008: http://daccessdds.un.org/doc/UNDOC/GEN/N02/309/14/PDF/N0230914.pdf? OpenElement

United Nations Security Council Resolution 1483, on the situation between Iraq and Kuwait, May 22, 2003. As of April 7, 2008: http://daccessdds.un.org/doc/UNDOC/GEN/N03/368/53/PDF/N0336853.pdf? OpenElement

United Nations Security Council Resolution 1510, on the situation in Afghanistan, October 13, 2003. As of April 7, 2008: http://daccessdds.un.org/doc/UNDOC/GEN/N03/555/55/PDF/N0355555.pdf? OpenElement

UNSC—*see* United Nations Security Council.

U.S. General Accounting Office, *Afghanistan Reconstruction: Deteriorating Security and Limited Resources Have Impeded Progress; Improvements in U.S. Strategy Needed*, Washington, D.C., GAO-04-403, June 2004. As of April 7, 2008: http://www.gao.gov/new.items/d04403.pdf

U.S. Joint Chiefs of Staff, Directive to Commander-in-Chief of United States Forces of Occupation Regarding the Military Government of Germany, 1067, April 1945. As of April 7, 2008: http://usa.usembassy.de/etexts/ga3-450426.pdf

Vaishnav, Milan, "Afghanistan: The Chimera of the 'Light Footprint,'" in Robert C. Orr, ed., *Winning the Peace: An American Strategy for Post-Conflict Reconstruction*, Washington, D.C.: CSIS Press, 2004.

Weinbaum, Marvin G., "Rebuilding Afghanistan: Impediments, Lessons, and Prospects," in Francis Fukuyama, ed., *Nation-Building: Beyond Afghanistan and Iraq*, Baltimore, Md.: Johns Hopkins University Press, 2006, pp. 125–144.

Wentz, Larry, ed., *Lessons from Bosnia: The IFOR Experience*, U.S. Department of Defense Command and Control Research Program and National Defense University, 1997. As of April 7, 2008: http://www.dodccrp.org/files/Wentz_Bosnia.pdf

White House, "The Clinton Administration's Policy on Managing Complex Contingency Operations: Presidential Decision Directive," white paper, May 1997. As of April 7, 2008: http://www.fas.org/irp/offdocs/pdd56.htm

Willoughby, Charles A., and John Chamberlain, *MacArthur 1941–1951*, New York: McGraw-Hill, 1954.

Woodward, Bob, *Bush at War*, New York: Simon and Schuster, 2002.

———, *State of Denial*, New York: Simon and Schuster, 2006.

Ziemke, Earl F., "Improvising Stability and Change in Postwar Germany," in Robert Wolfe, ed., *Americans as Proconsuls: United States Military Government in Germany and Japan, 1944–1952*, Carbondale, Ill.: Southern Illinois University Press, 1984, pp. 52–66.

———, *The U.S. Army in the Occupation of Germany, 1944–1946*, Washington, D.C.: U.S. Government Printing Office, 1990. As of April 7, 2008: http://www.history.army.mil/books/wwii/Occ-GY/

Zink, Harold, *The United States in Germany 1944–1955*, Princeton, N.J.: D. Van Nostrand Company, 1957.